AF588544

animal soul affirmations

Walking with Two Shadows

TALES OF LOVE, LOSS, AND REUNION FROM BEYOND THE RAINBOW BRIDGE

MARGO BOWBLIS

Published by:

animal soul affirmations
27 Dogwood Trail • Kinnelon, NJ 07405
Email: animalsoul2006@aol.com
Visit us at:
www.walkingwithtwoshadows.com

To purchase copies of this book,
contact the publisher above.

Printed in the United States of America

Produced by:
White Oak Editions, Seaman, OH 45679
cartaino@aol.com
Carol Cartaino, editor

animal soul affirmations

DEDICATION:

This book is dedicated to everyone in the front lines of the battle against animal cruelty:

...To my vet, Dr. Malathy Rao, and all the vets who practice kindness as well as good medicine, as well as all the vets involved in the fear-free veterinary movement.

...To Dr. Kara Seiford, who once again went way beyond the call of duty for me and my dog.

...To the rescuers who risk their lives evacuating animals from abuse, neglect, and Mother Nature.

...To the legislators who fight for animal rights.

...To the corporations who do the right thing regarding humane treatment of animals.

...To the researchers who understand we do not have the right to inflict horrible suffering on anyone or anything in the name of science.

...To the farmers who practice humane farming.

...To the trainers who train with kindness.

...And to the pet owners—I prefer the term guardians—who think of their animals' quality of life and needs, not just their own, in the way they treat their animals.

We are honored to announce that *Walking with Two Shadows* is the recipient of a finalist award from -The Eric Hoffer Award, as indicated by the seal on the cover.

"The Eric Hoffer Book Award is one of the largest international book awards for small, academic…and independent presses. The Hoffer Award recognizes excellence in publishing…" -Goodreads

AUTHOR'S NOTE:

For those of you who have older copies of *Walking with the Shadow of Love,* the female Labrador named Shango in that book was actually the same dog as the male Labrador named Cooper in this book. We had to change his name and gender in the first book due to a publishing issue that no longer exists. But we want you to know that Cooper was the puppy that Lakota and Zeak formed a lifelong bond with. One of Cooper's owners used to say that, "Lakota and Zeak taught Cooper how to be a dog."

And at the end of that book, it is Cooper who leaves the comfort of his owners to jump into the back of the car to console his buddy, Lakota, and be with him on the long ride home, after the loss of their beloved leader, Zeak, and the life-altering occurrence that happened as he was dying.

This book continues their stories, as they struggle to move forward without "The Zeakie Dog." We are updating the first book to align with the second book, now that we are free to use Cooper's name and identity, and we will be doing the same with our website.

Finally, we have searched for the highest quality photographs to tell our story. These photos are authentic narrative depictions of events in the book that were taken, at the time they were happening, with whatever devices were on hand. In some cases, the only photos available for specific events were very old and not of the highest quality. We have chosen to include them because they are an integral part of the story.

ACKNOWLEDGEMENTS:

My most sincere gratitude:

...To Carol Cartaino of White Oak Editions, who helps me to tame the wild horse of my writing into acceptable prose.

...To my brilliant and compassionate vet, Dr. Malathy Rao, who worked wonders with Lakota with cutting edge stem cell and PRP (platelet-rich plasma) treatments that kept him able to live his life to the very end doing the running, jumping, and swimming that was so much the joy of his beautiful spirit. And when the end came, Dr. Rao gave of her time to help me make the most agonizing decision faced by people who love their animals: When is it time to let go?

...To (in alphabetical order) Elizabeth Ahearn, Valerie Kerwin, Laurie E. Krauss, Cathy Lapenter, Patty Lapenter, Tom Lapenter, Jr., Tom Lapenter III, Samantha O'Neil, Tracy Quinn, Donna Riley, and Sheryl Spreen, for sharing their pet's beautiful stories with me to use in this book.

...To "Matt's" parents for reliving the pain of losing their son in order to share with me the poignant and beautiful story of "See You Again." I am grateful and honored for their trust in me to tell Matt's story, and their sharing of precious photographs.

...To Bill Bowblis for his technical expertise, without which this book could not have been created.

...To Dr. Richard Silvestri for his steadfast support in my life and in making these books possible.

...To all who contributed their photographs to this book: (In alphabetical order) William Bowblis, Valerie Kerwin, Laurie E. Krauss, Cathy Lapenter, Matt's mother and father, Kimiyasu Mizoo, Samantha O'Neil, Donna Riley, Sheryl Spreen, Sandra Struble; and to Dr. Rao for the use of her haiku.

...To all those who granted the right to use photos of their beloved family members and pets: Valerie Kerwin, Joan Krantz, Laurie E. Krauss, Cathy Lapenter, Patty Lapenter, Tom Lapenter, Jr., Tom Lapenter III, Matt's mother and father, Samantha O'Neil, Tracy Quinn, Donna Riley, Sheryl Spreen, and Sandra Struble.

...To Charlie Ebers for making a great connection for this book.

...To Sandra Struble for her input on some of the delicate decisions made for the book: Her insight and judgment were a guiding light for me during this process as they are in my whole life. You are truly my soul sister.

...To Sandra, Suze, and Reenie, for being the glue that holds me together when I begin to come unstrung, and the light that makes me laugh when I need to.

...To Inky, Cinder, Santana, Lakota, Zeak, Kaya and Maya for your ever-present, unconditional love.

TABLE OF CONTENTS:

BEYOND THE RAINBOW BRIDGE:

Awakened from the deepest sleep, I am no longer at your side. The hands that fed me, gave me water, groomed me and loved me are nowhere to be found. Before me lies the greenest grass, the bluest sky, and the clearest day I have ever seen. I arise to move forward, bracing myself for the terrible pain that my old body felt every time I had to stand, and to my astonishment, I freely bound upward, running, jumping, and…flying!

As I move forward, I see a cloud approaching. Wait…it's not a cloud…it is taking form…many forms. As it gets closer to me, I see it is composed of all my animal friends I remember from my life with you…and many, many, others I remember from before I was with you. They greet me and we run and play and drink the clear water and eat the abundant food that is provided—there is no need to hunt or kill. We communicate our thoughts and feelings telepathically—we are all happy, peaceful, and content. Only one thing keeps this beautiful place from being paradise: We miss the loving guardians with whom our souls bonded when we were in the physical world. We realize that we who are here, are here because we had achieved the deepest, most loving attachments… attachments so strong, that although we see the shining, rainbow bridge before us—and we are invited to cross over into paradise—we choose to wait.

Wait for you. Wait for you. We wait for you…and you only.

I can hear you in my heart. Every word you speak. Every thought in your mind. I feel your pain when you miss me. I feel some peace as you heal, but never stop loving me...never stop missing me...never forgetting me. I am there with you as you look at my pictures, and take walks where we used to walk. I am there with you in joy and I am there with you in sorrow. I wonder if you can see me, hear me, or sense me... or just know I am with you somehow.

Time here passes in an instant, though it may be many years in the physical world. Then a day comes when I can't hear you anymore...but then I see you... coming toward me...running, jumping, and...flying! No space separates us now. Warm tears of joy fall on my face as I feel your beloved hands caressing my head, my ears, my face...rubbing my shoulders, scratching my back just where I like it...together again. Finally. At last.

And now we walk toward the gleaming, arched, prism before us. We can hear each other's thoughts—feel each other's feelings. The ache is gone. The longing is fulfilled. We glide, crossing over...BEYOND the Rainbow Bridge...to home, each retaining our unique essence that makes us who we are and makes us recognizable to one another, while we are...

Together. Together. Together.

We are everything.

We are everyone.

We are every thought.

We are every prayer.

We.

Are.

LOVE.

The events that surrounded Zeak's passing were extraordinary.

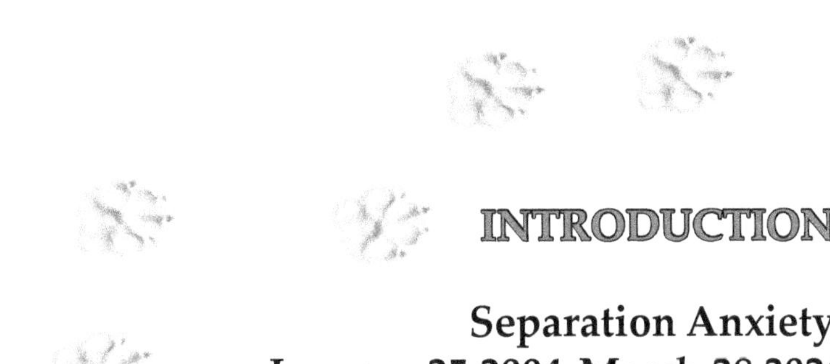

INTRODUCTION:

Separation Anxiety: January 25 2004-March 28 2026

I'm Margo Bowblis and I am an animal empath. An empath is someone who is "wired" differently: We are very sensitive and can detect things that most people can't. I didn't know this until my dog Zeak died and I had a profound, spiritual experience as he was leaving his body. The story of that is detailed in my first book: *Walking with the Shadow of Love*. Before that happened, I was a retired middle-school art teacher. But when Zeak—or The Zeakie Dog, as he was called by some of the seniors he visited as a therapy dog—came into my life, everything changed. It was as if my whole life reverted back to my childhood passion, which was animals.

On Monday March 28, 2016, Lakota (registered name: Lakota-Margo's Shadow) crossed over the Rainbow Bridge. He was the one-in-a-million-dog that I was lucky enough to be blessed with for twelve years and three months. Those of you who have read *Walking with the Shadow of Love* know about the first half of his life. But there is more to Lakota's story than that.

Empaths are an example of people whose brain and body chemistry causes them to experience things in ways that others cannot. These are interesting anomalies that we are just beginning to learn about. One of these is synesthesia, which causes senses to be paired. A musician who sees colors when he or she hears music would be an example of this. I had a student in my class once who "tasted colors." Mirror-touch synesthesia causes the person who has it to feel the physical sensations of others. For example, a doctor with it would experience all the pain sensations of his patients. Imagine how valuable this condition could be to a pediatric health care worker who had patients who couldn't tell them what hurts. It would also be a great help for a veterinarian. But this ability can be hard on a person, because it is difficult to live with.

When my other dog, Zeak, first came to me, Lakota had stepped back—it was as though he knew Zeak would only be with us for a short time. He let Zeak have everything he wanted: toys, treats, chew toys... even me. It was unusual for an adult, male dog to let a puppy come into his home and take over everything. Lakota was a very confident dog, high on the pack leadership scale. It was puzzling.

When Zeak died, it was Lakota who pulled his broken owner through. The events that surrounded Zeak's passing were extraordinary, and although they came to be a great source of comfort down the road, they left me in a state of shock for quite a while. At my side the whole time was Lakota—always. He became much more overtly affectionate. He slept snuggled up to me at night and followed me everywhere. He guarded and protected me. He made me play—every morning, whether I wanted to or not—thus lifting my spirits and helping me to recover. As we recovered from the loss we had both sustained, our bond grew deeper.

Lakota was not only my personal therapy dog during this period. His visits to people in hospitals and nursing homes and assisted living facilities brightened their lives for eleven and a half years. By the time his life was done, the people he had visited numbered in the thousands. He was the dog that was allowed to visit the most fragile patients because he was so trusted…so calm…so loving and gentle. We called him "Dog Buddha." He was my rock and my compass…he steadied me and guided me on my life path, at times when I was unsteady.

The people in these facilities would have been shocked to see Lakota's other side. All it took was someone throwing a stick or a tennis ball into the lake we lived by and often walked around, or firing the tennis ball gun in our back yard, and Lakota turned into a wildly athletic field dog. He would fly into the lake, shooting a massive wedge of water out from his sides, and then settle down to his fast, powerful swimming stride. He would get to his target, whip his "otter tail" (a special tail that Labradors have) around to execute a quick turn, and glide back to me with his treasure. He would drop it at my feet with pride…unless it was a "really good" stick, in which case he would chew it up.

It was unusual for an adult, male dog to let a puppy come into his home and take over everything.

This duality of calm therapy dog/wild field dog was at least partially because he was a hybrid Labrador. He was the product of an accidental breeding. I will say more about that later, because even though it produced the perfect balanced Labrador, it also caused some problems. He would tear through the woods at top speed, jumping over trees and off of big rocks. His athleticism was a beautiful sight to behold—a magnificent animal expression, full of joy, vigor, love, and passion. I held my breath on these romps, but it was his true nature to be so free and to push the limits of his body. The only way I could have contained it would have been to make him spend his life on the end of a leash, and that would have broken his spirit.

As the time passed, away from the extraordinary event that took place as Zeak was dying, Lakota and I experienced many contacts from Zeak. I have included some of them in this book. As Lakota grew older, I found myself wondering if I would have contacts from him after he crossed over. I believed that The Zeakie Dog was a highly advanced soul, and wondered if Lakota would know how to "come though" to me. I feared the pain would be unbearable if I lost touch with him. I had never been aware of contacts from my other dogs. Maybe I wasn't evolved enough to detect them, or maybe they were younger souls and didn't know how to come to me. Maybe, I wondered, Zeak was extraordinary, and only he could do this. Or maybe, Zeak had done something to me in those life-altering last moments of his life; something that has made me able to detect spirit now...something that would enable me to detect Lakota. It was that theory that felt right to me and comforted me, because not long after I lost Zeak, I also lost my mother, and I had three separate contacts from her after she crossed over. These kinds of things were not happening to me before Zeak passed.

I finally got answers to these questions in a book called The Empath's Survival Guide, by Judith Orloff, MD. I now know that I am an animal empath, and that is why I can sometimes detect my beloved pets' spirits. When I was a child, I never wanted to play with dolls. I only wanted to play with toy animals or real animals. I enjoyed and loved my human friends, but my private time was always about animals. Dr. Orloff, who is a psychiatrist and also an empath, says about ten to fifteen percent of the population are empaths. That is why only some of us can detect spirits, hidden emotions, undetected illness, and/or Earth events such as earthquakes and tsunamis.

It is not easy being like this. We are easily hurt and vulnerable. If you are reading this and suspect you might be an empath, I strongly recommend Dr. Orloff's book because it will give you coping strategies to help make life a little gentler. It also contains tests to determine if your suspicions are correct: whether you are indeed an empath. I wish it had existed when I was young—I could have saved myself a lot of misery.

I am deeply grateful to Dr. Orloff for writing this book and taking the incredibly brave step of revealing that she is also an empath. She has helped a lot of us to understand ourselves better. But some heartaches cannot be avoided, and one was coming at me faster than I was ready for. I was just beginning to heal from the last two losses. It was too soon for another.

As Lakota's journey unfolds in this book and he reaches the end of his time here, I must again face the devastation of losing a dog that I have an extraordinary bond with. And, as you will see, I get the answer to my question as to whether or not I will have continuing contact with him. I also get to find out if the images I am seeing are really "there" in the room with me, or just in my mind's eye, after experiencing something called an "afterimage." I also experience the protective reaction many people express—fear of having to go through this pain again: "I don't ever want another dog because I can't bear to go through this again."

I cancelled all of my author appearances for *Walking with the Shadow of Love* as I grieved. How could I work without my partner, who was the heart and soul of these gatherings? My health took a nosedive. And that was how I felt for four months, until one Friday afternoon when my spirits moved me to take a bold step very suddenly. In that moment, I knew without question that a life without a dog was not the life I wanted to live anymore. The reader will follow, with me, the light path (this is a term used to describe a spiritual intervention) that led me to rescue a dog I named Kaya on that fateful afternoon and begin the process of saving her from the damage of her past. I had no idea what a challenge it was going to be at the time, but it has been so rewarding to save a life and help a dog who had many of the same issues that I have. I believe that is why I have been able to help her, and why she has been able to help me.

Due to Lakota's health problems I only had a chance to do a few book events before his passing. He had delighted audiences and warmed them up, and everyone in attendance had fallen in love with him. As I met and spoke to people at these encounters, I heard more and more from people who had experienced contacts from loved ones who had passed—both human and animal. Some had never told anyone for fear of being ridiculed or judged in a negative way. Now sometimes the stories come to me from other sources, because people are becoming more comfortable with sharing such encounters, and I have included some of them in this book.

I now know that it is my purpose, for the rest of the time I have here, to spread this message. I would like people to feel comfortable speaking up about their experiences, providing yet more evidence that animals are evolved, spiritual beings who go on in a different form after they leave the physical world. I can only hope that making this information more available will help to put an end to the awful abuse and torture of helpless animals at the hands of people who do not understand this. I also seek to comfort those who have lost their beloved pets and let them know that their animals do go on and are even around them. While the majority of people are unable to detect their pets who are now in a spirit form, the ten or fifteen percent of us who happen to be "wired" so we can detect them, want people to know those beloved pets are there.

I hope to spend the rest of my days sharing my love and connection to animals with others, depicting the beauty of animals and nature with my work, and most important of all, helping Kaya to find peace, feel loved and secure, and experience fun and joy. She is so deserving of those things.

Margo Bowblis

One of the most beautiful things about Lakota was his generosity. He would share anything he had with anyone he loved.

CHAPTER ONE:

After The Zeakie Dog Has Departed: December 2011

I had never been aware that I had any psychic abilities. I am not a puppy, so you would think if I had these kinds of tendencies I would have noticed it by now. So how do I go forward after having a life-altering, mind-blowing spiritual event that rocked my world, changed my focus, and totally altered my concept of reality? The short answer is: My dogs will lead the way.

It has been a few months since the events I recounted in *Walking with the Shadow of Love* occurred. My beautiful black Labrador, Lakota, and I have been grieving the loss of The Zeakie Dog together. If I had to go through this alone, I don't know if I would make it. As usual, Lakota has been my rock. I have sensed him really stepping up to give me more love, affection, and support to help me though this terrible loss.

I had never experienced a bond with anyone or anything like I had with Zeakie, after he came into my life. To begin with, meeting a puppy who belongs to someone else, and experiencing such an instantaneous, undeniable connection that it results in the young dog screaming when you leave, is unusual. But when this connection actually manifests in the dog becoming yours, when you have no intentions of having a second dog, it is completely out of left field. And then, later on, just when I thought cancer had taken him from me, he revealed himself to be an invincible spirit, who would never leave my side. It all left me overwhelmed.

In between the unexpected beginning and the extraordinary end, Zeak was a therapy dog who could flip the mood of a room full of people from sorrow to joy in a second. As we did this important work, to suddenly be told that your dog—at age four—has a deadly cancer and will be gone in days—maybe a week—is akin to having an anvil dropped on your head. The truth is, from the time I got the terrible news, until the time Zeak crossed over into the next life, I spent fifteen months fighting the battle of my—and his—life, so I had no time to process what was happening. Then, as he was leaving his body, we shared an experience that shattered every boundary of reality I had experienced in my years on this Earth. So I am not ashamed to admit that I was completely knocked off my center.

What happened on that, the last day of his life here, was the beginning of a new understanding, for me, of the nature of the boundaries between the physical and the spiritual. I learned what powerful beings our animals really are once they have left the physical world. Since that day, I have had regular incidents of some kind of contact from Zeak. They have all been different, unexpected, and always incredibly uplifting, since that fateful day—11/13/11.

One of the most common types of contacts I have with Zeak involves seeing his shadowy form out of the corner of my eye, while I am simultaneously sensing the mass of his body there. Sometimes I have to alter my path to avoid stepping on him and I assume it's Lakota; but then I see Lakota is sleeping on the far side of the room.

These visits and contacts assume many forms. My husband is science-oriented and was initially a skeptic. For that reason, I was delighted to have Zeak include him—much to his surprise--in two of his visits. It happened as follows:

It was right around the third anniversary of Zeak's passing. Bill and I were going to Costco, but as it turned out, we weren't going alone! I drove to Costco and Bill drove home. On the way home, right in the middle of an unrelated conversation, I had an overpowering feeling that there was a big, black dog in the back seat. It was so intense that I stopped what I was saying and turned around to see what I could clearly feel was there. It was a powerful feeling, but I didn't see anything. I couldn't shake the feeling, so I turned around a few more times, but still I didn't see anything. I told Bill, who was silent. A few minutes later, he admitted to me that on the way down, when I was driving, he had the same thing happen. He felt the presence of a large black dog so intensely that he turned around several times to see if what he was feeling was there.

The next day, he was working in my room, fixing an electrical connection on my salt lamp. Much to his surprise, out of the corner of his eye, he saw a shadowy image of Zeak.

Another thing Zeak does is send me symbols. He was black and white, and he sends me black and white butterflies behaving oddly. One day when I was hiking with my friend Elaine, a black and white butterfly landed on my hat and stayed there for the entire half-mile down the mountain. When we reached the end of the trail, it flew off. I have had one land on my windshield right in front of my face at a red traffic light and fly off just before the light changed. They have followed me and landed on me more times than one would ever expect, and preceded me on hiking trails, as though they were leading me.

Zeakie also likes to leave me stars. I find them in unexpected places, popping up out of nowhere. They are on the ground right in front of me in the woods, in my house, on the road by my house, in songs at significant times, and in graphic, high-definition dreams that include him surrounded by stars. One of my favorite star incidents was a synchronicity involving a childhood book. As defined in Wikipedia, "Synchronicity is a concept, first introduced by analytical psychologist Carl Jung, which holds that events are 'meaningful coincidences' if they occur with no causal relationship yet seem to be meaningfully related."

Bill and I were driving to the park with Lakota to hike on our favorite trail. As we were driving up the steep hill to the entrance, for no reason at all, a quote popped into my head from a book I had read many, many years ago. The book was The Little Prince *by Antoine de Saint-Exupery. The quote was: "And now here is my secret, a very simple secret: It is only with the heart that one can see rightly; what is essential is invisible to the eye." I said the quote aloud to Bill, wondering why, after all these years, I should remember that quote, completely out of context.*

That evening, we decided to look for a movie to stream on Netflix. Imagine my surprise, when the moment we tuned in Netflix an ad came on for a brand-new movie made by Netflix: a new version of The Little Prince. *Needless to say, our choice of what film to view was being directed for some rea-*

son. So we watched it, and as I watched, I got the touching message of how being a caretaker can deepen love, and our understanding of the eternal nature of spirit. And, much to my surprise and delight, there were stars everywhere! Stars were a major theme of the movie, and at the end, there was a star hanging in the middle of the screen to remind me who sent me a beautiful message, by directing me to watch this movie.

Perhaps one of the more interesting aspects of these events is that I wasn't going through this alone...Lakota was indicating, in different ways, that he was experiencing these contacts, too. He followed things that I could not see around rooms, air scenting. He had never done this before Zeak passed away. He woke up suddenly from sound sleeps, and appeared to see something and follow it into my room. And these shared phenomena, coupled with his increasing affection, expressed more and more overtly, added to the increasing bond I was feeling with Lakota, now that he wasn't being overshadowed by the powerful presence that was the energy of The Zeakie Dog.

When we speak of someone's "energy" here, we are not just talking about their vim and vigor. In the context of spirituality, energy has a different meaning. Because I am an emotional empath I can sense energy. In this case it means a feeling of someone's "essence." I just think of that person and I get a sensation that is unique to them. When my mother came to me after she passed, I knew it was her immediately—even before I got a visual image—because I could feel her. I believe that this is how we recognize one another when we meet, after we depart the physical world and enter the spiritual realm or heaven. I have also heard from my spiritual teachers that our energy contains everything we have ever experienced. Try closing your eyes and thinking of someone close to you. Do you get a unique feeling you associate with that person or animal? If you do, then you are sensing their energy.

One of the most beautiful things about Lakota was his generosity. He would share anything he had with anyone he loved. His friends could play with his toys, get treats or affection from me, and be fed alongside him and he never objected. He was a strong, confident dog, and yet when Zeak was a puppy, he allowed him to take things out of his mouth, without protesting. He was a loving, generous soul, as illustrated by the following anecdote.

Every Saturday we went to a local dairy for ice cream. Lakota and Zeak came along, and each one got a tiny cup of soft-serve vanilla ice cream. (The soft serve was actually ice milk, so it was low fat enough that the small amount they were given was fine.) The dogs LOVED this weekly treat! It might have been their favorite food, and they might have passed up a steak in favor of it! Zeak used to eat his with his eyes closed in ecstasy. Lakota loved it so much that before I could even give it to him, drool poured out of his mouth in surprising amounts, necessitating something we called "the slobber towel," which was an old beach towel we put under the dogs to keep the large puddle of drool off the car seats and floor.

On one of these trips, we had the car set up with the slobber towel in place, and my husband and I each had one dog's cup of the treasured treat in our hand: Bill had Zeak's and I had Lakota's. We counted to three and held the cups out to the dogs. The frantic licking began, and Zeak's tongue must have been moving faster because he finished first. Before we could react, and without skipping a beat, Zeak plunged his nose into Lakota's almost-empty cup. Most dogs would have objected strenuously to another dog invading such a treasured and limited resource, but not Lakota. He shifted to the side to give his adopted brother more room to share that last lick. And that's how it was between these two male dogs.

And so it was with touching, but tearful, memories that we got in the car for the first time after losing Zeak, with only Lakota, to make our Saturday pilgrimage to the ice cream dairy. It was a scenic drive there, passing through preserved farmland with horses and alpacas grazing on both sides of the road. Fall was just about done with its colorful display, but the green and amber fields, the dramatic clouds, and the animals still made for a beautiful view. It didn't matter, because I cried most of the way.

It was an unusually warm day for November—warm enough that we decided to have our ice cream on one of the benches on the sidewalk outside of the dairy. This always made things easier, because it eliminated the need for the slobber towel. The slobber just became part of the pâté of ice cream drips, chocolate and rainbow sprinkles, and other spilled things on the sidewalk. I stayed outside with Lakota, and Bill went in to get the goodies.

Because Lakota was a therapy dog, people would often ask if their children could say hello to him when they saw his tag. I was always happy to accommodate them since Lakota loved kids, and it was an opportunity to educate the children about how to behave around dogs. Today was no different, and when the parents of a little girl asked if she could pet Lakota, I was happy for the distraction from missing Zeak, and said that would be fine. The child was gently petting Lakota and getting some wet kisses from his big tongue, when Bill came out with our ice cream. It was too late to tell him to go back—Lakota had already seen him and knew very well what was in the bag he was carrying. I explained to the little girl that Lakota was *very* anxious to have his treat. She then asked if she could give him his ice cream.

I tried to warn them—I really did! I looked at her parents and told them that, while Lakota would be very careful and gentle with their little girl, this would not be a neat process. I explained about the drool to them and to the child, but they were all determined that she would enjoy this special experience since they did not have a dog. Bill handed Lakota's ice cream to the girl and she held it out for Lakota.

The problem with this was logistics: When we fed Lakota ice cream he was downhill from us because we were taller. This little girl was downhill from Lakota! The difference this made was, that as she held the cup up to him, rivers of ice-cream-tinged drool started pouring down her arm, running down her pretty pastel dress, and then dripping onto the sidewalk. Once this process had started, it was hard to stop, because Lakota just kept following her, licking all the while, as she tried to move away. It wasn't going to be over till it was over! It stopped when the ice cream ran out. To her credit, the child wasn't all that bothered by it, but her parents—not being used to dog drippings—were horrified. We got the slobber towel and some antibacterial wipes and cheerfully offered them to the squeamish parents. They cleaned their daughter up as best they could and moved on…quickly!

It was a welcome distraction for me, and it was always uplifting to see how gentle and loving Lakota was with children. I said, "gentle and loving"—I did not say "neat."

For those of you trying to reach out to your animals who have crossed over, I would like to share what I know about this experience. I know beyond a show of a doubt that telepathic animal communication is possible because I personally experienced it as Zeak was dying. It was real. It was as clear as if it were in writing. It was conversational. That does not mean that everyone who says they can communicate with animals is legitimate. I caution you to be careful and mindful in your choices. I have dealt with people I know are legitimate and at least one phony.

Just when I thought cancer had taken him from me,
he revealed himself to be an invincible spirit
who would never leave my side.

*They would lie together "in pack"
and share a toy or an antler.*

CHAPTER TWO:

The $1800 Play Date: December 2011

There was no knock or doorbell, just the squeaking sound of the front door opening ever so slowly. And just as slowly a big, black nose squeezed its way through the cracked-open door, into the living room, followed by a furry black head, an equally furry black body, and a thick, black otter tail. It was in this manner that Lakota's best buddy and fellow black Labrador, Cooper, entered our home, followed by one of his owners, my neighbor Elaine.

As Cooper was making his entrance, Lakota's larger, black furry body was poised and ready for the attack, but he did not utter a sound. He was stationed in his sentry position at the end of the couch, with his head low and his eyes in the fixed stare of a predator, locking gazes with the "intruder." Cooper returned the intent gaze and even added a tacit "Nya-nya-nya-nya-nya—you don't scare me one bit!" The staring contest went on for over a minute. Anyone who did not know what was about to happen would assume these two were canine gladiators, about to engage and fight to the finish of one of them.

I was perched in my recliner but did not get up to greet my neighbor at the door, nor did she come to greet me. Instead she ran for her life to the couch and tucked her legs up on top of it while I, just as quickly, wrapped my legs around me on top of the recliner—it was the only way to protect ourselves from the two big dogs clipping our legs as they ran by, and setting us up for what would surely be a knee replacement. We knew it was just a matter of time. If the recliner and couch had seatbelts, we would have buckled them. The show was about to begin!

It was impossible to tell who started it. It was literally as though the two dogs had both been shot out of a rocket launcher! Cooper was running full speed around the couches, cornering like a Ferrari, with Lakota in hot pursuit. Round and round the couch and recliners they ran, with occasional route changes around the sides of the coffee table in front of the couch. It was impossible to fathom how they could run so fast and corner so hard in our living room. If we had any kind of flooring other than wall-to-wall carpet, they would have been seriously injured. And that is exactly why I didn't have lovely hardwood floors like my friends all did.

It always ended the same way—Cooper would drop to the floor and say "uncle" and Lakota would dance over him and feign putting his jaws around him—but never closing them. There would be all sorts of growling noises, drool, and kicking involved. If the windows were open, I often wondered what passers-by thought was going on in our home. When Zeak was alive, he was part of this, too—all ninety-six pounds of him.

The dogs would catch their breath for a few minutes. Then Cooper would give his buddy a "Yes, sir—I totally respect you and will never make sarcastic eye-contact with you again, sir..." Then, he would walk around the couch, lower his head, and do exactly that. If he could have, he would have thumbed his nose at Lakota, who was mumbling in dog-language something to the effect of: "C'mere, you little #*@%!" And with that, it would start all over again.

Nobody ever lost their temper. Nobody ever got hurt. The control these dogs had of their jaws was amazing. It was all an elaborate game, with many variations. It was incredibly macho, dare-me, oh-yeah? posturing at its most hilarious. When they had enough of chasing each other around the furniture, the second stage of the game would kick in: the toys.

Phase two would began when Cooper picked out a toy from the toy basket, shook it at Lakota, and said something in dog language to the effect of, "Ha ha, bro...I have your toy. What are you gonna do about it?"

At this point, Lakota would chase Cooper again, round and round the furniture until he caught him, and take back his toy. Sometimes, Cooper would try jumping on the couch to keep his prize, but that never worked; and on more than one occasion, it resulted in Elaine or Allie, Cooper's other owner, having the two big dogs tugging at the toy on her lap. Lakota was considerably larger and more dominant and competitive than his mellow, easy-going buddy, so it wasn't really a contest—he always got the toy. However, what happened next was surprising. Lakota would lie down next to his pal and give him the toy. Sometimes it was a stuffed toy—sometimes an antler (a commonly used chew stick for dogs,) but whatever it was, once Lakota had it back, the next thing he wanted to do was share it with his best buddy. And this is where the "bromance" began!

What happened next was what I referred to as the "decompression" stage of the play date. They needed to catch their breath, so they would lie together "in pack" and share a toy or an antler. After they had a chance to recover, they usually moved into the "explosion" phase. This usually involved a tug-of-war with a toy until it exploded. White, fluffy toy stuffing shot all over the living room, as they ripped and tore the pieces of their "kill." Then they shook the pieces violently, as if to be sure every last bit of stuffing was strewn on the carpet. Sometimes it would just be one toy—sometimes it would be several of them. When they were done, it often looked like there had been a blizzard in our living room.

One would think that would have been the end… but it wasn't. Cooper still had some tricks up his sleeve. Sometimes he would grab a piece of a toy and run out the dog door, with Lakota in hot pursuit. We didn't allow the dogs to take the soft toys outside because they would get dirty, and we couldn't leave them out there because they would get moldy. Lakota knew that, and followed that rule religiously. But his buddy didn't live here, so he decided he was exempted from that rule. Lakota believed it was his job to see that Cooper obeyed the "no inside toys outside" rule, and the fact that it fit in with his definition of great fun made it even more delightful. So the game moved outside. This allowed Elaine and I to put our legs down so the blood could resume circulating in them again.

We could even grab some coffee or a cold drink and then watch the boys tearing around the yard outside as clods of grass were kicked high into the air and long skid marks dug into the sod. Eventually, Lakota would get the toy back and bring it in the house, but not before the two dogs had run out every last bit of their energy.

One afternoon, Cooper came up with Allie for a play date. The dogs went through all of their normal antics, and during the "explosion" phase, the tug-o-war involved a large toy that got ripped up and gutted in the usual manner. The two dogs then became fixated on a piece of fabric with a plastic lining that had formed the bottom of the toy. Lakota had it, and Cooper was chasing him all around trying to get it. For a moment I thought about taking if from them, because it had gotten so slimy and wet that I wondered if they could possibly swallow it. I inspected it, but it was so large I didn't think it was a problem, and they were having s-o-o-o-o much fun with it, so I gave it back. The fun and chasing continued until I noticed the toy piece was gone. Allie and I launched a search party. I even called Bill in to help move the couch. We looked everywhere, but the missing toy part was nowhere to be found.

I had thought it was much too large to be swallowed, even by a large dog. It was an oval about five by seven inches and had two layers: fabric and a thin plastic. The longer we searched and couldn't find it, the more worried we became. It was beginning to look like one of the dogs had eaten it…but which one? Or had we just failed to find it?

We decided to keep looking, but still couldn't find it. It was now too late for a trip to the vet. I fed Lakota, hoping if he had eaten the toy, he would throw it up. But he didn't. He was normal all night. We all went to bed, still wondering about the missing toy piece. Early the next morning we got up, and a few minutes later, Lakota threw up a small amount of foamy white saliva on the rug. That did it. I put him in the car and took him to the emergency vet.

At the emergency vet's, they felt his stomach and took him for X-rays. The X-rays were inconclusive. They showed some stuff in his intestines and some bubbles, but that could just be food or gas. The vet asked me if I was sure Lakota had eaten the toy. I said that the only proof I had was that the toy had disappeared, we couldn't find it anywhere, and it had been seen in Lakota's mouth. Lakota almost never had stomach issues and he had thrown up some foam. That was enough evidence for me to decide to bring him to the vet.

The emergency vet suggested I take the X-rays to my own vet when she opened, and see how she wanted to proceed, so I did. At Dr. Rao's, we were all concerned about the plastic part of the toy not being digestible. But we didn't want to put Lakota through anesthesia and surgery to find out unless he showed more conclusive symptoms. My vet suggested we do a barium swallow X-ray. It might show something that the regular X-rays didn't. And even if it didn't, the barium might push out the toy as it worked its way through Lakota's digestive tract.

Those of you who have read *Walking with the Shadow of Love* know that this was not the first time Lakota had eaten something he shouldn't have. In fact, when I had bought health insurance for him, the representative had said, "I see you have a Lab. You'll be happy to hear that this policy covers accidental ingestion." But right now, I was too terrified of Lakota having an intestinal obstruction to think about such things. I just wanted that toy out of him.

The next day, during our walk, the white barium poop happened, and *another toy that we had no idea Lakota had eaten came out!* But the missing toy did not. Ever. Maybe the blessed event happened while Lakota was so far away in the woods that I never knew it happened. Maybe it was in him for the rest of his life and caused no problems, although it seemed that would be impossible, given the size of the object. Maybe gnomes took it and he never swallowed it. Maybe a doggy miracle happened. I will never know. When all was said and done, the vet bills were in excess of $1800. Thankfully, insurance covered eighty percent of the bill. Even so, all in all, it was one very expensive play date!

Then Lakota hit his stride, cutting smoothly through the water like a speedboat-- even leaving a wake behind him.

CHAPTER THREE:

Work Ethic: November 2012

On October 29, 2012, Super Storm Sandy rocked us to our core. We sat in our old lake house, seriously wondering if the roof was going to be torn off. Massive trees were uprooted all throughout our community, including one in our back yard that could possibly have killed us all if it had hit our house. Fortunately, it spared our house and our barn and just took out a section of our fence. When it was over, we were once again, as we had been in some past storms, trapped in our lake community for over a week. There was no power and no way in or out. Eventually, crews got to us and the sound of chainsaws and wood chippers became the norm for a couple of weeks. By the third week in November, we were once again fully functional.

It was a rainy afternoon and I was working up in the loft. I hated it when I had to work up there because I knew Lakota was upset by it—at any given time, he wanted to be with me. He would just lie at the bottom of the ladder for hours till I came back down. I felt so guilty leaving him there, but we could not afford to put an addition on our home, so this was the only space we had for an office. I regretted every minute I spent away from him, but I had no other choice.

Lakota would wait there for hours, silently, patiently, and tirelessly till I was done. When I came down he would give me a full-out greeting, as though I had been out of the house the whole time. On this particular day, it was raining so I was working inside and my dog was doing what most dogs do on rainy days: dozing. So, it was a surprise to me when I heard him bark. Just as moms everywhere know their baby's cries and what they mean, I knew Lakota's barks. This was not his, "Someone's here." bark. It was not his, "A dog is going down the street" bark, either. I wasn't even his, "That darn, brown, UPS truck is here and the guy in it is trying to get into our house, again!" bark. Instead, this was his, "Something's wrong and I'm worried—you'd better get down here right away!" bark.

I knew not to ignore this urgent message from this very intelligent dog, so I climbed down the ladder to see what was going on. As soon as I hit the floor, Lakota led me over to the fireplace. His demeanor was that of Lassie leading a search party to find his beloved Timmy, who had fallen into a well. I became anxious, fearing a giant spider or some other scary intruder. But arachnid home invasion was not what had my dog so concerned. What Lakota was barking at was a leak: a slow trickle of water dripping down from where the roof met the chimney.

Most dogs would have ignored this or not even been aware of it. But this dog had such a fierce work ethic that he would let me know if the slightest thing was out of place. I had experienced this many times with insect awareness. I am seriously allergic to bee stings. If there was a bee in the house, Lakota would let me know. I am also bug-phobic. If there was a spider or a cricket in the house, he would let me know. He even would inform me if there was a tick on the rug. I had long appreciated this service, which he provided for me twenty-four seven! But now, he was letting me know about this tiny leak, which I might not have even noticed until it did real damage.

My son repaired the flashing on the roof the next day. Lakota was truly my guardian, and I felt safe and secure with him around. He always had my back! And he was not only my guardian—he was my helper. His favorite words were, "Help Mommy" because he knew that would be followed by a job, and he passionately loved to work. "Work" assumed many forms for Lakota. Fetching the newspaper from the mailbox, getting me my slippers, picking up things I dropped, and searching for, finding, and retrieving things; all fit into the definition of "work" for my dog. Lakota's work ethic was not confined to the house. It extended to everywhere he went, and sometimes he was so zealous that he may have stepped on others' toes—or paws.

One particularly sunny, warm, autumn morning, we set off on the trails around the lake where we lived. My intention was to take Lakota for a romp in the woods and a nice swim. We hiked around the lake to the first dog swimming area, and my water-loving Labrador glided into the water. I threw sticks for him to retrieve until my arm ached, and my boy still wanted more. I called for him to come out, and, for the sake of my aging rotator cuff, decided to burn up the rest of his energy in the woods.

We hiked further around the lake until we came to one of the large beaches. Our lake allowed dogs on the beaches in the off-season, and the dogs loved racing in the soft sand and enjoyed the lake, even in the spring and fall and winter. Lakota was just approaching the water when an athletic, young man with a pitching arm like a major leaguer arrived on the scene with a pair of hyperactive, field dog, chocolate Labradors. Their owner told me they were littermates and were three years old. Lakota was two months short of eight years old. For a Labrador, this was senior-citizen-hood, but nobody had told Lakota that.

Lakota saw the tennis ball leave the man's hand and he blasted his way into the lake, sending two huge wedges of water shooting out on either side of him. Then he hit his stride, cutting smoothly through the water like a speedboat—even leaving a wake behind him. He streaked past the two chocolates until he reached the object of his obsession: the tennis ball. The two young dogs never had a prayer. Lakota then swam the ball in, evading the chocolates' attempt to wrestle the ball from his mouth, and dropped it at my feet. I returned the ball to its owner.

This sequence was repeated several times. During this time, neither of the young Labs ever got near their ball. Their owner noticed the grey hair on Lakota's chin, and asked how old he was. When I told him, his jaw dropped. I decided that Lakota had exercised enough. Lakota disagreed, so I leashed him and led him away so the two younger dogs could actually play with their ball. To Lakota, retrieving that tennis ball was his job, and nobody was going to stop him from doing it well.

Fall did not gently morph into winter: It hit a huge white wall, in the form of an early snowstorm. Lakota and I had been snow hiking on the trails with my neighbor and her dog, and we were almost home. We had just reached where the trail ended at the bottom of our street, when my neighbor noticed her glove was gone. She told me she was going to have to go back down the trail to find her glove. Several other neighbors were outside talking, and they heard me tell my friend, "You don't have to go—Lakota will get it for you." A couple of the guys joked with me saying, "Seriously? You've got to be kidding!

I had never asked Lakota to go to retrieve something for anyone else before, and never from so far away. But I often dropped my gloves while trying to deal with dog treats and leashes, and I had to keep my hands warm, because I had Reynaud's Disease. Anytime I dropped a glove or anything else, Lakota automatically picked it up and brought it to me. So I was pretty confident he would understand what I wanted him to do, and he l-o-v-e-d to help! I had him smell my neighbor's other glove, and then asked him to "go get it." He disappeared down the trail and was gone for a few minutes. I was beginning to get a little concerned when my neighbor—who was quite a bit taller than me and could see farther down the trail—shouted, "He's running down the trail and--can you believe it—he has my glove in his mouth!" Lakota actually got applause from the neighbors witnessing this that day. I was so proud of him, but for Lakota, it was all in a day's work. He proudly dropped the glove at my feet and I gave him a treat and a hug. As I walked home, I marveled at the intelligence of this dog, in that he could make the mental leap from picking up something close by to travelling a long way back in the snow to find a lost glove. To me, it was just one more illustration of how much we underestimate the intelligence of animals, simply because they don't speak the same language we do, and have different priorities than we do.

We would be horrified at the arrogance of anyone who assumed that anyone who spoke a different language than they did was less intelligent. And yet, we make these kinds of assumptions all the time about animals. I remember being told in school that one of the differences between humans and animals is that only humans used tools. We now know that there are several species of animals that use tools, some of them quite surprising: Birds and octopuses come to mind. I believe that our low expectations of animals' intelligence are self-fulfilling. People who assume their dogs are not capable of learning or communicating don't challenge them to do so or spend time teaching them. Dogs actually understand our language much better than we understand theirs. Lakota understood English to a very large degree. He just didn't speak it. Because I put a lot of effort into communicating with him, I had learned to understand his language better than a lot of people understand the language of dogs. And it had just paid off handsomely in getting the glove-retrieval job done and making quite an impression on our neighbors.

When the World Trade Center came down,
a call went out for dog/handler teams
with this high level of certification to go to Pier 94
in New York to work with the Red Cross Workers,
the Police, and the other first
responders who were doing the traumatic work of
dealing with the disaster firsthand.

CHAPTER FOUR:

Flash: Several Years Ago

In Walking with the Shadow of Love, *I told the story of my two therapy dogs, and some of the work they did. I am continuing that story in this book, with Lakota and Cooper. There are different kinds of therapy dogs, and some of them require special training beyond the normal certifications. They are called Disaster Stress Relief Dogs, and they work under very demanding conditions. This is the story of one of them.*

Donna Riley is a dog trainer by profession. For some time, she had very much wanted an Australian Shepherd. Through a professional contact, she met a breeder of exceptional quality dogs. When she visited, there was a litter, but all of the puppies had been spoken for. She told the breeder how much she wanted one of her puppies, and was put "on the list" for the next litter.

When the new puppies were born, she was able to see them at just two days old. She visited them several times after that. She knew she wanted a male, and she was drawn, at first, to a large male. The breeder also suggested the larger of the two males that were available, because it was more suitable for show. Donna was leaning towards the show-quality puppy, but the smaller one, who was the runt of the litter, kept catching Donna's attention and coming over to her. The breeder was letting Donna make the choice and Donna was feeling a connection with the smaller pup.

On the day she went to get her puppy, the smaller male was the first to come to her. The breeder asked her which puppy she wanted. Donna told her that her eye was going to the larger puppy, but her heart was going to the runt. And so, Flash came home with her. Surprisingly, he grew to be the second-largest puppy in the litter. The breeder was happy when Donna chose him. She was hoping Donna would take that puppy, because she could see the instant bond between them.

When Flash was about a year and a half old, he became sick. He had a string of issues and several vets didn't know what was wrong. The sickness came and went, and one day when they were working in an obedience class, the trainer said that someone's dog must have split a nail because there was blood on the floor. Everyone looked their dogs over, but found nothing. A few minutes later, there was more blood on the floor. This time, Donna found blood on Flash's chest. She noticed him licking his nose, and discovered his nose was bleeding badly. But he had just kept on doing his job and hidden the problem—the kind of stoic behavior that is an admirable characteristic of herding dogs.

It took several vets and many tests before one of the vets figured out what was wrong. Flash had deep lesions inside his nose. The cause: an autoimmune disease called Discoid lupus erythematosus. The vets believed he got the disease because his immune system attacked his body due to a vaccine reaction.

The vet put Flash on Prednisone and he reacted badly to it. Donna took Flash to a board-certified internist who treated Flash with Erythromycin and a nutritional supplement called Niacinamide, and he responded very well. But they told Donna that, because of the lupus, Flash would be an old dog when he was only seven years old.

Flash went on to win several obedience titles and also to become a therapy dog. It was the therapy dog work that Flash loved the most. Donna decided that since Flash was so good at that type of work, they would take the Disaster Stress Relief Therapy Dog Test, a test requiring a higher level of training. He passed the test, and they moved forward with more therapy dog work.

When the World Trade Center came down, a call went out for dog/handler teams with this high level of certification to go to Pier 94 in New York to work with the Red Cross workers, the police, and other first responders who were doing the traumatic work of dealing with the disaster firsthand. The teams had to be approved by F.E.M.A. and they were given special permission to take the dogs on the ferryboat to cross the Hudson and get to their destination. As Donna and Flash did this difficult work, the close bond between them deepened even further.

They went in twice a week—that was the maximum amount of time they were allowed to do this stressful work. Donna liked to say that she held the leash, but Flash "did the magic." One of the groups they worked with was a group of children of missing people who were believed to still be lost in the rubble. They were there with family members who had been summoned to bring samples that could be used for DNA matching, to identify victims. The children were in a nursery, and were so traumatized that they would not speak to anyone. But they talked to the dogs, pouring out their feelings. The Red Cross workers also sat with, and talked to, the dogs. Clearly, the dogs had a healing effect on the people they worked with...the "magic" Donna spoke of.

But some of the first responders needed something different from the dogs. A group of police officers who had been doing the grim work of looking for bodies on the site came to the center to have lunch and, after interacting with the dogs for a while, asked the handlers if they could go outside with the dogs. There were autumn decorations on the tables, and the police brought a few of the miniature pumpkins out on the dock and were enjoying having the dogs fetch them. After all the sorrow and the trauma the officers had been facing every day, what they needed the most…was to play.

The time after this passed all too quickly, as it does for all of us when it comes to our dog's lives. Despite what the vets had predicted, Flash was now just short of fifteen years old. Flash had been getting sicker. The lupus he had battled for most of his life had been flaring, as well as some other issues. Donna's vet had done everything that could be done in the way of medical intervention, and nothing was helping.

One morning, when Flash went downstairs, he couldn't get back up the stairs because he was weak and in so much pain. Donna went over to him, and when their eyes met she knew: knew that he had become so sick that quality of life was no longer sustainable. She settled him down on the porch so he didn't have to move. Then she called her vet and told him that "it was time." Knowing how special Flash was to her, he suggested she bring him in at lunchtime so that there would not be any other clients there. He asked if the dog was too uncomfortable to wait the hour until lunchtime, and Donna told him it would be OK to bring him in at noon.

She then went and sat down on the floor with her dog. She spoke with him as one would speak with a person, because when we spend time talking with our dogs—as I said before--they may not speak our language, but they understand a lot more than some people think they do. She told him that she knew he had been hanging on for her, but it was too hard for him and it was time to go. He sat up and raised his head—looking upward towards the only gap in the trees that allowed sky to peek through—and let out a loud, happy-sounding bark.

Donna's eyes followed the direction that Flash was looking in, as she sat on the floor with her arm around her dog. As she slowly turned toward the gap in the trees to see what he was looking at, she saw a "translucent, watercolor" version of Flash leave his body and run up toward the gap in the trees. Before he reached the open space, the spirit body turned and looked at Donna. "It's OK...go...you can go!" she said. The spirit body turned to look at her a second time. Then the same loud bark came out of Flash's physical body, and he slumped to the ground...and was gone.

Donna called her vet and told him, "You're not going to believe this, but Flash just died in my arms." The vet told her he was not surprised to hear that. When she arrived at the vet with her dog's body, he told her that the reason he was not surprised was that Flash had been so sick, that he was surprised he had lasted this long. He believed that the dog had held on, waiting for Donna to be ready to let him go.

After that day, Lakota never, ever got into the car with a light heart again-- even with his buddy with him.

CHAPTER FIVE:

The Blizzard: January 2012

I leave my Christmas tree up for a week after January first. I love how it looks and I'm not in a hurry to lose its lovely glow. During the first week of January 2012, I decided to go pick up my mom and bring her to our house for a visit. I had made an apple pie and knew she would enjoy having a piece with coffee, by the fire, with the tree up, before I took it down.

My mom lived in a lovely, assisted living facility about twenty minutes from my house. She lived there because she had some degree of dementia and needed to be in a safe environment. She had done well on her own until she reached ninety. Soon after her ninetieth birthday her dog passed away. The loss hit her hard, and she began to have difficulties.

My brother had made some adaptations to her home to try to keep her safe, because she was adamant about wanting to stay there; but she had two accidental fires in the kitchen, and the second one was serious. Since she lived in the next state, we couldn't just drop in and check up on her; and she had refused to move closer when we discussed it with her. When I brought her to my house to visit, she had to be watched constantly. If she ventured into the kitchen with the gas appliances, or wandered near the steep, dark, basement steps, it could be a disaster in the making. It was much like having a toddler around, only one tall enough to reach everything.

My brother and I explained to her that she needed to make the move for her safety and because she needed to be closer to us. It was hard for her at first, but she adjusted nicely, liked living where she was now, and had friends, and great food, and entertainment. However, coming to visit her kids trumped all of that. The weather forecast that morning said that a snowstorm was coming around seven p.m. Since I was picking her up around eleven a.m. and planned to bring her back around three, I saw no need to disappoint her by cancelling our plans. I put Lakota in the SUV and took off. I told my mom we would get there a little early so Lakota could do a therapy dog visit and cheer up the other residents—who weren't coming to my house for apple pie and a last dose of Christmas cheer.

We arrived on time, Lakota did his job well, as he always did, and I got my mom ready to leave. I noticed she didn't have gloves, so I asked her where they were. She didn't know, so we lost quite a bit of time searching for them. When we couldn't find them and time was passing, I told her to wait by the front door and I would pick her up in the heated car.

We drove home and enjoyed a lovely lunch together. I perked a pot of fresh coffee—I am a lover of percolated coffee because it is so much better than drip coffee—and we sat down to enjoy homemade apple pie à la mode. We were just finishing our pie and coffee when something caught my eye out the window: *white*!

It was only two o'clock. How could they be so wrong about the time of the storm's arrival on the same day it was happening? I knew the weather was not always accurate a day or two before an event, but the same day they were this much off? They had meteorologists. They had electronic maps. They had radar. For cryin' out loud, they even had satellites. How could they possible mess up this badly??!! I would never have picked up my mother if I had suspected this could happen.

Keeping her at my house overnight was not an option. She had to get back for medication administered by the nurses—medication she could not miss. I would also have to stay up all night to be sure she wasn't setting our house on fire like she had her own…twice. I decided to leave with her immediately.

I wasn't concerned about driving in snow. I used to ski and had a lot of snow driving under my belt. My SUV was very competent on snow, and I also had equipped it with snow tires so I could get through snow if I needed to, for whatever reason. I put my mom in the car and Lakota gave me his "Please don't leave me." Look, so I put him in the SUV, too. Off we went to make the twenty-minute trip.

It was truly a winter wonderland. The flakes were sticking to everything. The trees were covered in snow and swaying in the wind. I put some Christmas music in the CD player, and encouraged my mother to sing along because she was a little apprehensive about the weather.

As we pulled out onto the long, winding road to her home, I felt out the road conditions. It was a little on the slippery side, but nothing my vehicle couldn't handle, especially with the snow tires. We were gently driving along in a breathtaking white world singing Christmas carols. We were a little less than halfway to her home, when I saw a vehicle coming towards us in the distance. The minute I saw it I knew it was in trouble.

The white car had come around a far bend on the winding road and gone into a very slow, very long spin. Because it was rotating it was taking up the whole road, which consisted of only one lane in each direction. I was wondering where to put my vehicle to get us out of harm's way. There was no shoulder. There was just the road and a slowly spinning car coming towards us. To make matters worse, it was snowing much harder, so I could barely see. I suffer from anxiety and panic attacks, but at that moment, something came over me: I was as calm as I have ever been in my life. I briefly thought of trying to go around the car in its lane because it was heading into ours, but rejected that idea. We could be hit by an oncoming car going even faster than this one. The skidding and spinning had somewhat slowed this one down. Plus, we wouldn't fit because the car was now coming down the road sideways, heading right for us, taking up both lanes.

The car was approaching fast and I had to decide…NOW. I remembered my older-model SUV was equipped with only front air bags. My decision—made calmly and logically for some other-worldly reason—was to maneuver my car so we would be hit head on, rather than from the side, which would have made my ninety-three-year-old mother take the hit. This way, the air bags would protect us…I hoped. I said a prayer to Archangel Michael, with whom I had always felt a special connection. There are people who would mock this, but I am dead serious about it. Then I asked Zeak to protect his brother, Lakota. From that moment on, time changed speeds.

Everything now was in slow motion. My mother cried out, "He's going to hit us!" I calmly told her to sit pressed against the seat back so the belt would tighten and hold her. I told her that the air bags would protect us. Lakota was wearing a thick, fleece-lined car seat-belt harness and was tethered to the seat belt anchor. I called the "down" command back to him, so the back of my seat would also help keep him from being thrown forward. I steered the car in a slight curve to line it up so that the impact would be with the front of the car. The impact came, and it was like hitting a giant marshmallow, really, really, really hard. And then there were a missing few minutes—a lapse like I wasn't there. I had no awareness of blacking out...my head didn't hit anything except the air bag so there was no head impact. It was as though something had removed me from the physical world for a short time. I was never aware of the airbags inflating—I only realized that had happened as I returned. I called to my mom, asking her if she was OK and she answered that she was. By now, the owner of the vehicle—a young man—was pulling at my door to open it and saying, "Oh, God—are you all right?" I said I thought I was OK, but my mom was ninety-three with a heart condition, and my dog was in the car and I couldn't see how he was.

The snow was coming down so hard none of us could see. I was terrified that another car would plow into us full speed. The young man who'd been driving the car that hit us was also not injured, and said he would call the police and went to do that. My mom was badly shaken and I need to get her to safety. I looked in the back seat in my mirror, and Lakota was back up looking around and seemed all right. I felt so helpless. We couldn't get off the road because there was nowhere to go because we were on reservoir watershed land and the road was lined with pine trees. And then, an angel—actually two angels—arrived on the scene.

A young man and his sister, who lived a few houses down the street from us and were actually friends of the person who hit us, were behind us in their SUV. They put their flashers on and moved their vehicle closer to the side of the road. Then the young man and the driver of the car that hit us forced my mother's badly bent door open and picked her up and carried her to their vehicle. Snow and ice were now lashing us to the point that it was painful. I untethered Lakota and brought him to their vehicle and we got him in—then me. My hands were burning because my gloves were back in my vehicle. My mother and I were shivering from the cold. Lakota was shivering because he was terrified. I hung onto them both.

The female of the duo who rescued us cranked up the heat and offered my mom her mittens. My mother put them on to help warm up her hands. I couldn't call my husband for help. He had a sports car that couldn't even get out of the driveway when it snowed. I don't know what we would have done if our young neighbors hadn't had come along and been kind enough to help us. My thoughts were interrupted by a flashing red light behind us. We could just make it out through the thick snow. I was relieved to see the police here. I was very worried about my mother and I wanted to get her home. I hoped the police would assist us.

In my life, the police had always been looked upon as help arriving. Most of the officers I had contact with were former students or my friends' sons and daughters. This was a different town, but I didn't expect things to be any different. So I was a little taken aback when the officer came to the vehicle and started yelling at me to give him my license and registration and insurance card. I got out and handed it to him. Like my mom, I have problems with staying warm: My hands and feet were on fire and I was still shivering, so it was hard to talk. I told him my mother was ninety-three with a heart condition and I was concerned about getting her home to her facility where she could be checked out and cared for. He responded by yelling at me again. I felt warm tears start to flow down my face. He was very rattled. It was dangerous for all of us to be stopped here with the visibility so bad. I kept my mouth shut and was glad when I could get back in the car.

After the officer got everybody's paperwork, he asked what had happened. The young man said very honestly that when he rounded the curve his car went into a skid and he couldn't stop it. He said that he then crossed the center line and hit our vehicle. He told the full truth. The officer asked me for my version, and I said the same. I told him that I believed it was the slippery road conditions that had caused the other driver to lose control of his vehicle, and that he and his friends had been very helpful and concerned.

This was not the accident scenario that our lawyers would have dreamed of! Nobody was trying to get away with anything. The driver of the car that hit us took responsibility for his actions. I had no intention of taking advantage of someone who was a victim of horrible weather conditions and who had been truthful about what happened, rather than keeping his mouth shut as his lawyer would have advised. I backed him up because I had not seen him do anything wrong. He hit ice and the rest was in God's hands. We were all blessed to be safe and sound.

My mother was confused. Her dementia, coupled with the stress of the accident, had her in a condition that warranted attention. I gingerly told the officer again that I needed to get her back to her facility for evaluation. I told him she was frightened, but I had no way to get her there. I told him there could be serious consequences if she didn't get her medication. At that point, the policeman must have realized how harshly he had treated us. He apologized, saying that there were accidents all over the place and the police were overwhelmed. I still had no way to get my mother to her residence, or myself and Lakota home. I asked the brother and sister in the SUV if it would be possible for them to drive us and they kindly agreed to do that. I thanked them profusely.

I sat next to my mom, with Lakota half on my lap, as we rode to her home. She insisted she was fine but was a little confused about what had happened. I told her the nurse would decide if she needed further care. I dropped her off and—after quickly advising the staff about the accident and asking them to take my mother to the nurse there—returned to the SUV quickly, not wanted to hold up my rescuers and allow the roads to get even worse. The young man was a very competent driver and he got us all home safely.

There is no doubt that there were damages. My mother and I had pain in the center of our chests from our seatbelts for a couple of months. My lovely, reliable, well-maintained small SUV had taken the hit for us, and was totaled. Insurance paid us what the car was worth, but in truth we lost thousands of dollars because we couldn't find another vehicle that age in as good condition, so we had to buy a newer used one for more money. It took almost a year for me to be able to drive without fearing cars coming at me from the other direction were going to hit me. But the worst damage from the accident was to my dog.

All through the ride back the night of the accident, I could feel Lakota tremble every once in a while. My unshakeable dog—the dog who could handle anything, the dog who had faced a bear, the confident, secure rock that I leaned on when I needed support—had been badly shaken. Lakota had always loved the car. Other than an occasional trip to the vet, the car always meant good things to him: rides to the dairy for ice cream on Saturdays, rides to visit my kids and their dog, Shy, trips to the pet store and the dog bakery, and riding to do therapy dog work. As far as Lakota was concerned, the car was a great place...until today. Outside of the car he was fine now. But the car being fun—even joyful—was ruined forever on that day, and "all the king's horses and all the king's men" couldn't put Lakota together again as far as the car was concerned. I worked at counter-conditioning him for the rest of his life, but after that day, Lakota never, ever got into a car with a light heart again.

CHAPTER SIX:

Spirit Images: January 2012

It was a viciously cold, windy, winter day, and Elaine and I decided to have an indoor play date with the dogs to avoid them (and us) getting frostbite. It was a rare day that we didn't go on our morning hike, but single-digit temperatures and a ripping wind were just too harsh and dangerous. Elaine and Cooper arrived at the appointed time and came in. Immediately, Lakota and Cooper—full of pent-up energy from missing their morning hike—started "The Game." As usual, Cooper tore around the living room, making occasional detours between the couch and the coffee table, with Lakota in hot pursuit. They ran until they were drained of energy and then collapsed and lay panting and trying to catch their breath. As soon as they did, another round began. This went on for about fifteen minutes until they were too exhausted to continue.

I had gone into the kitchen to make coffee while some of this was going on. I called the dogs into the kitchen for "cookie time!" and gave them each a treat. After their snack, the two of them settled down in front of the fireplace for a nap and I brought out the coffee and some homemade chocolate chip cookies (yum!). As we indulged in our treats, we couldn't help but notice and be touched by how the dogs were cuddled together as close as they possibly could be. It was not cold at all in the house and they had been running, so it was not for warmth that they were pressed against one another. It was affection—an expression of the loving bond between these two dogs, who once had been a pack of three, and now had only each other. It brought back memories of the days when Zeak was still with us and all three dogs would lie together like this.

As we were enjoying the dogs, the coffee, and the cookies, Elaine picked up her phone and snapped a picture of the dogs to save the moment. After she took it she opened it to see if it was to her liking. She perused it for quite a while, and then asked me to come and see it, saying, "Margo, come and look at this!" I went over and sat next to her on the couch, wondering what could be so interesting in this photo that we couldn't already see looking at the dogs. What I saw in the image made the tiny little hairs on my arms stand up and tingle.

In the picture, along with Lakota and Cooper, was a white, wispy, hint of a third figure. I could just make out the faint outline of a long, Zeakie nose and his two big stand-up German Shepherd ears. I immediately started looking for explanations. The sun was low in the west and none of its light could get to the part of the house where the dogs were lying, so it wasn't a sun flare. There was no reasonable explanation for the image in the photo. And this wasn't me initially looking at this and making this connection—it was Elaine who noticed something in her picture—something we couldn't see looking at the two dogs with our naked eyes.

I asked her to email me the picture so I could blow it up for a closer look. When I enlarged the photo, I could see more clearly that the faint, white cirrus-cloud-like image bore a striking resemblance to The Zeakie Dog, puppy-piling with

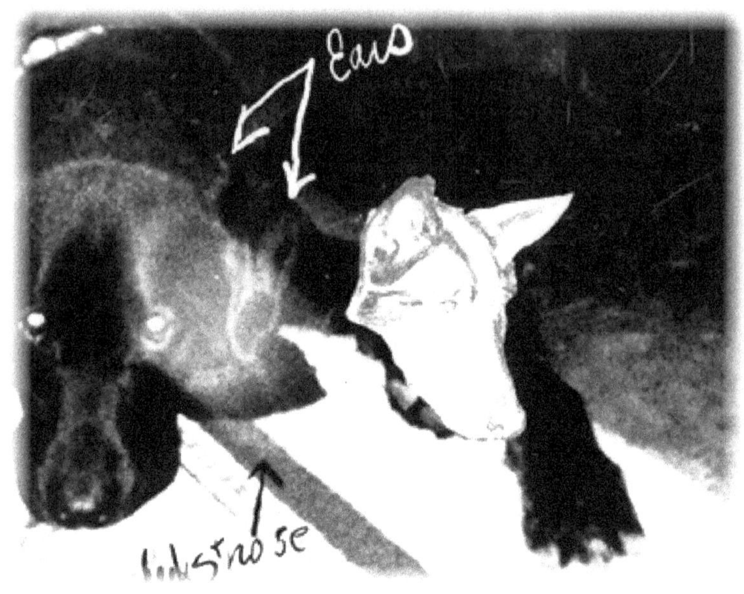

In this photo, I have cut and pasted a picture of Zeak's head on the right side of the picture to help the viewer locate the misty, white Zeak head shape in Elaine's photo. Because this has been transferred and copied it is hard to see the image, but it is still somewhat recognizable if you compare the white shape to the pasted head to the right.

The top photo is my picture of Zeak.
The bottom photo is Elaine's picture
Printed on top of my picture in one
pass of the printer.

his two buddies, just as he would have if he were there in his physical body.

So many times since Zeak had passed, he had left us assurances that he was still around—existing, just in a different form. I was convinced that Lakota could see him more clearly and more often than I could. Many of Zeak's contacts had been preceded by Lakota following something around the room. Lakota was one of the most solid, confident, intelligent, un-neurotic dogs I have ever known. That was why he made such a good therapy dog. He could handle almost anything. This was a physically, neurologically, and cognitively sound dog. It was reassuring to me that Lakota was sensing the same things I was. This was new territory for me, and he was leading the way for me.

After I had finished looking at the enlarged photo, I saved it in a folder in my computer with other pictures I had taken in January of 2012. I entered a description of this event in the journal I was keeping of contacts from Zeak. I thought that was the end of this—but it wasn't.

It was a rare day that I didn't use my computer at all. I always checked my email, and I was doing a lot of writing—writing that eventually lead to the creation of Walking with the Shadow of Love. *I was also going through thousands of photos—deciding which ones to keep and which to purge. I had printed a dozen or more documents and used all of the functions I normally used on my computer, several times. So when I went up to the loft to work on my computer two weeks later, it had been used a lot since I looked at Elaine's picture and I had not opened that picture or looked at it in any way, since. There was absolutely no earthly reason for that picture to make an appearance, without me going to the folder it was in and opening it. There was no reason for me to do that, since I had printed it out and had it in my room, where I didn't have to climb a ladder to look at it.*

On this particular day, I went up to the loft to make a print of a picture of Zeak that I had taken back in 2010 and wanted to frame. Since I had at least one new folder of photos a month—and sometimes more if there were special occasions—the folder I opened with the picture of Zeak that I wanted to print out was nowhere near the one with the picture Elaine recently took in front of the fireplace. I did not click on anything but the folder from 2010. It opened immediately and I clicked on the picture I wanted: an image of Zeak smiling. I tweaked the colors and contrast a little and printed out a full-page-sized photo of the picture. That was what was on the monitor. That was what I printed. That was not what came out of the printer. Once again, as I had the other times things like this had happened, I could feel chills run up my arms.

What came out of the printer was the large, full-sized image that I had taken back in 2010 of Zeak smiling like the Cheshire Cat from Alice in Wonderland. But that was not all. Superimposed on top of that image was printed the picture that Elaine had taken with the ghostly image of Zeak in it. I had not opened that picture in weeks. And now, here it was, mysteriously printed on top of Zeak's grinning picture. I had opened many other folders and printed many documents and pictures between then and now, so it couldn't have been left in the queue or it would have printed out before all those other documents and pictures. And how could it have printed itself on top of another image?

I called Bill, who was an electronics technician, to ask him that question. He was the one who always solved my computer enigmas. His explanation was as follows: "That could not have happened—it's impossible. First of all, you say you didn't open that picture. Second of all, it printed on top of the other picture. There is no way it could have done that."

But it did.

There appears to be some kind of connection between spirits and electricity. I have witnessed numerous incidents involving electricity that I believe are contacts from my animals. To the best of my memory, things like this never happened—not even once—before these animals passed. Flickering lights at significant times, electric candles turning on—never off, and once, even our gas fireplace switching itself on right in front of me, are the type of things that I believe are visits. A woman wrote into my blog to say that after her dog died, a screen saver with the dog's picture kept popping up on her computer when it had no reason to come on the screen. She had a strong sense that it was her dog visiting her.

The air was crystal clear, and the tender green glow
of the distant trees combined with
the blue sky and water presented
a delicately colored view of emerging spring.

CHAPTER SEVEN:

A Leg to Stand on: May 2012

Every once in a while, my friend Donna would come over with her pack for a hike and a swim. It was with that particular intention that we set out on this Spring morning; but our hike was destined to be a short one.

Donna, her three Aussie Shepherds, Lakota, and I started down the trail at the end of my street. We hiked through the woods to the dam, walked over it, and admired the panoramic view. The air was crystal clear, and the tender green glow of the distant trees combined with the blue sky and water presented a delicately colored view of emerging spring. The Earth was coming back to life, and the dogs were ready to celebrate this and were full of excitement.

After crossing the dam, we started back through the meadow and headed for the lake trail. The dogs were tearing through some tall grass when Lakota suddenly stopped and let out a blood-curdling scream that made my heart stop. It went on for a good minute: screams, yelps, crying, and general sounds of pain…agony, and no clue of what had happened. As we made our way towards him, Donna gave voice to the same thought running through my own mind: We were both wondering if my boy had been bitten by a poisonous snake. I also feared another awful scenario: Could someone have set one of those horrible leg-traps in the woods?

But there was no snakebite or leg trap when we reached Lakota. Instead, we found him standing on three legs with his left front leg held up off the ground. He was still crying—now softly. It was the first time I had ever heard my dog cry out in pain, and it was killing me to see and hear him in such misery. Dogs hide their pain, and I knew it would take a lot to make my dog cry out like this, so I was terrified of what we were going to find.

We gently and carefully examined his foot and leg. There was no clue on the outside of his leg or foot what the source of his pain was. But whatever it was that was causing his distress, it was serious enough to prevent him from putting his leg down. So it was very slow going—a few feet at a time on three legs, then rest—till we finally reached where the trail ended and the road began.

Donna and her pack stayed with Lakota and I went home and got my SUV and my wallet. I drove to the end of the road and, with Donna's help, put Lakota's car harness on. Using the harness to partially lift him, we managed to get him into the vehicle, and I headed for the vet while Donna and her dogs headed home.

At the vet's, it took very little time for the vet to home in on the problem: Lakota's left front elbow. She took X-rays and came back with a diagnosis. She said that my boy had elbow dysplasia. There was a string of long words after this proclamation, but the bottom line was that my dog had been born with a malformed joint in his elbow, and his athletic romps were tearing it to pieces. It would "go out" like it had today from time to time until...her voice trailed off as she said this. Swimming was the best, safest, exercise for him. She gave him a steroid and a painkiller. He had to rest it until it was better and go easy on it for the rest of his life. And so, my dog—who didn't know the meaning of "go easy" on anything—didn't know it, but had just had his wings clipped. How could he live a quality life? He was an athlete. Everything he loved to do involved running, jumping, or swimming, and it looked like two out of three of those activities were now forbidden.

After this awful injury in the woods, I expected Lakota to slow down. I had underestimated my boy. Once the flare-up had calmed down, he pretty much went back to business as usual. Sometimes dog owners have to make hard choices. If I kept him on a leash for the rest of his life, he would be less likely to have a painful incident like the one he had. However, his elbow would continue to degenerate, and the picture down the road was not good, even if I kept him on a leash. On the other hand, if I did keep him leashed, he would be miserable, depressed, and lose the fabulous conditioning of the rest of his body. Lakota was an unusually fit Lab for his age. He was solid muscle, with very little fat on his body. That was working for him. I could not possibly leash-walk him enough to maintain his current level of fitness.

Because my dog was on the high end of the intelligence spectrum, I suspected that he was already self-managing his injury by carrying most of his weight on the other front leg. Dogs carry most of their weight on their front legs—roughly seventy percent. The problem with that was, we had no idea if that leg had the same problem. The vet had told us there was a good chance that it did. If it did, the extra weight on that leg was going to cause problems down the road. A dog with bad back legs can use a cart that holds up the back end—kind of like a dog wheelchair. But front leg carts were very difficult to use. Most of the dog's weight would be on them and they are very difficult for the dog to turn. For that reason, a dog with two bad front legs was often done. I couldn't even think of something like that happening to Lakota. He was too vibrant, happy, energetic, and full of life. There was no surgical fix for this at this point in time. I had asked the vet.

Elbow dysplasia was just beginning to show up in Labradors. When breeders select for certain traits, they inadvertently add others. It's kind of like when Congress tacks an unrelated item onto a bill. When the bill passes, so does the other item—which may be something undesirable. Lakota had been an accidental breeding—the breeder had been up front and ethical about that, so this trait might not have ever shown up in her normal line. I had searched the Northeast for a hybrid: half retrieving field dog and half show, or bench dog as it is also called. I was not a fan of either of the two extremes that breeders had taken Labs to: Many pure field dogs were too hyper and many pure bench dogs were lethargic and it was very hard to control their weight. With his field dog mom and his bench dog dad, Lakota was the perfect dog for me: loving, intelligent, athletic but not hyper, strong, healthy, loyal, loving, obedient, and endowed with that incredible work ethic. However, all these wonderful traits had a hitchhiker: elbow dysplasia.

I decided to defer to Lakota's intelligence and see if he could manage his elbow problem and still enjoy his freedom. And so, for now, I gave my boy permission to live his life—the life he loved—until he could no longer do that. How far down the road that would be was anyone's guess.

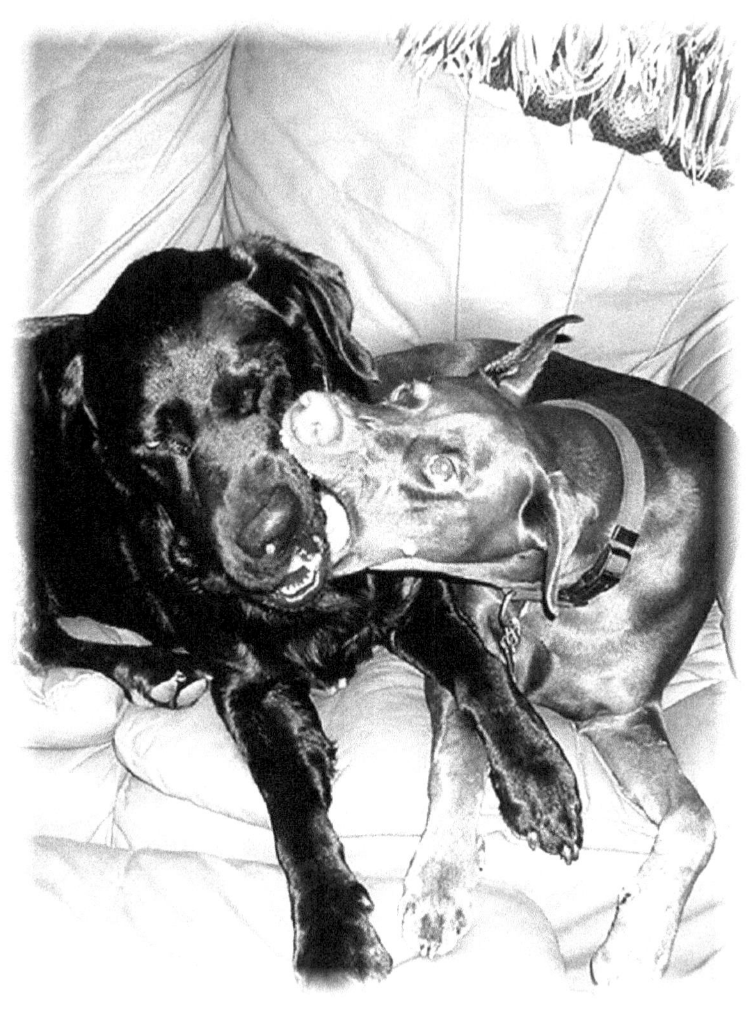

With that single action, she thereby declared,
"I'm in charge here now."

CHAPTER EIGHT:

Shy's Explosions: July 2012

My granddog, Shy, was one of the quirkiest, funniest, most fiercely protective, bossy, obedient, super-affectionate dogs I have ever known. That's quite a string of adjectives, some of which may seem contradictory, but they all applied. Shy was short for "Shy Ann", keeping with our family tradition of Native American dog names, but with some spelling liberties taken.

Tom and Pat had decided on a Doberman puppy after a bear tore down their fence, came into the yard where my young grandson regularly played, and broke into the crawlspace of their house. In that crawlspace were the washer, dryer, and freezer. So they had to go down there frequently at different times of day and night. They needed an uber-vigilant guard dog that would alert them and my grandson if there was a bear or a coyote anywhere near their house. And they got exactly what they needed in Shy.

When they went to the breeder to pick out a puppy, they took my young grandson with them. They all went into a room with the breeder and all of the puppies and their mom. They sat on the floor to just observe and discuss the different personalities in the litter. But, as it has always been in our family, the choice was made by the dog—not the people.

As they sat on the floor, the smallest female in the litter immediately went over to my grandson. And there she stayed. I believe that dog knew she was to be his guardian. And there just wasn't any arguing with that kind of conviction, so instead of taking what they had come for—the biggest, strongest pup in the litter—they took the smallest pup, who had attached herself to my grandson like a girl on a mission...because she *was* a girl on a mission.

She grew up to be a beautiful dog. Golden-red, she had amber eyes with lime green rings around the pupils. She was the alpha female in every way with other dogs and with strange people, but with her family she was obedient, loving, funny and—did I say quirky? We were part of her pack, so when she came to visit us, she was the same way.

Zeakie weighed ninety-six pounds. Lakota weighed eighty-two pounds. Shy weighed sixty-five pounds. When she walked in the door of our house, the first thing that happened was she went over to Zeak and Lakota and opened her petite but alligator-like mouth as wide as she could and put it around each of my boys' muzzles, one after the other. With that single action, she thereby declared, "I'm in charge here now." Despite their larger size and the fact that it was their territory, neither of my boys ever argued with that. "Yes, Ma'am," they in effect said.

The second thing she did when she came to our house was to run in and out of the dog door into our fenced-in yard—about twenty times. She l-o-v-e-d the dog door. Ogden Nash once wrote, "A door is something that a dog perpetually wants to be on the other side of." He was right. With the dog door, Shy could be on the other side of the door all the time. And so she was, back and forth, in and out.

Shy was constantly on duty. I had trained my boys to be minimal barkers, so as not to disturb my neighbors. But Shy had a job to do at home in the rural area where she lived, and she couldn't turn it off when she came to our house. To Shy, every living thing was a life-threatening menace, and she produced lots of loud, shrill barking. So as soon as it started, I would have to close the dog door and bring her in. But that wasn't enough to stop it. The barking would continue inside and at ear-splitting levels. I finally had to resort to something I called "sensory deprivation." I closed every window, pulled down every shade, and closed every curtain in the house. It was dark and gloomy, but it was…q-u-i-e-t. Thankfully.

When we had our dog party gatherings, Shy was a fan favorite. She would approach every person there, lean up against them, and stay with them till they got tired of petting her, massaging her, and scratching her back. Then she would move on to the next person. With the dogs, she was super friendly, but not quite so gentle.

Shy played rough. She would "soft bite" my boys' necks as they ran and played, but she didn't do it gently enough, and they began to avoid running with her so they didn't get roughed up by her. There were exceptions. Shy always played gently with puppies, up until they were about two years old. It was said that she gave them a "puppy pass."

Watching her play with Cooper was particularly funny. Cooper appeared to think Shy was a "hottie." When he came over, when she was at our house, he would flirt by looking her in the eye, shaking his bared teeth at her, and then running like hell! The chase would go on until Shy almost caught him, at which point, Cooper would take a dive, roll over on his back and say, "Yes, Ma'am—I was only kidding, Ma'am."

My grandson and I spent many lovely days in the woods with Lakota, Zeak, and Shy, watching them tear around the trails. On one summer Sunday when the weather had turned warm, my boys turned onto the trail to the dog beach at our lake, and I figured why not let them go for a swim. Lakota and Zeak plunged into the water while a stunned Shy watched from the shore. A lot of Doberman Pinschers don't swim. It might be because they are so lean and muscular that they don't float, so they have to work pretty hard to swim. But this was a *huge* problem for Shy. As the self- appointed pack leader/alpha female, she obviously believed she had to be able to do everything the other dogs could do; and do it better, faster, and longer. There was just no getting around it for her: Shy had to learn to swim.

She eased into the water and started to paddle—faster and faster and more and more frantically—until a twelve-foot geyser of water shot up in front of her as she paddled along. The problem was, she was trying to keep her whole front end out of the water. It was so funny we were all doubled over, and the whole thing started to attract a small group of pointing, laughing people. Then an amazing thing happened: Lakota glided up beside her and gave her an actual swimming lesson. Being a Labrador, Lakota was an expert, powerful swimmer. He saw what the problem was and wanted to help Shy. He pulled up next to her and spoke with her in short, loud, very high-pitched barks—a sound I had never heard him make before. Shy must have understood what he was communicating, because she immediately settled down lower into the water and started gliding through the water like a pro, with Lakota by her side. From that day on, she was a strong, fast swimmer who maintained her leadership. But with that, we had a problem.

The canine gene for OCD (Obsessive-Compulsive Disorder) was first discovered in Doberman Pinschers. We now know that many breeds can develop this disorder, but "Dobies" were the first to be recognized with a gene for it. I mention this because once Shy had mastered swimming, she discovered dragonflies. And once she discovered dragonflies, she became obsessed with them. Any time we took the dogs swimming, if there were dragonflies in the area, the normally obedient Shy would zone out and obsessively start paddling after the dragonflies, determined to catch one. Instead of swimming and fetching sticks like the other dogs, Shy went off on her own dragonfly hunt and would not come back. It wasn't exactly disobedience, because I don't think she even heard me. She was so focused on her obsession that all of her senses were turned off. After a day where it took us a ridiculous amount of time to get her out of the lake, I decided I would need to keep a floating line on her. A floating line is a rope that floats on the surface of the water so it won't tangle in a dog's legs while they ae swimming. It worked beautifully, because she was so obsessed with following her prey that she didn't even notice it was attached to her. When we were ready to go, we grabbed the end—which we had tied to a tree—and just reeled her in like a big fish.

At this point in the story, I am going to insert a warning. I am assuming that if you are reading this you are a dog person or an animal person and, as such, you have long gotten over being squeamish about bodily fluids. But if you are easily grossed out, you may want to skip this section on go on to the next chapter.

One of Shy's unique features was her digestive system. It didn't act up often, but when it did, it was tumultuous. To illustrate this, I present the following two incidents.

My kids had invited several couples over for a barbecue, including us. It was the time of year when acorns start to fall, and this particular year there was a bumper crop. Acorns are toxic to dogs, and can also perforate their digestive systems with their sharp points and the sharp edges left when they are chewed and swallowed. Unfortunately, no one could convince Shy that this was the case—she *loved* them and would eat them any time she could. More than once I had pried her jaws open to remove them, and getting Shy to open her vise-like jaws was no easy task. But on this particular day we were all socializing out in the yard and not paying attention to acorns. Shy seized this opportunity to chow down on them.

When it was time to eat, we all went into the house. We were gathered around the kitchen island and Shy was lying on one end of the sectional in the living room. Suddenly a loud sound made us all turn toward the source: Shy was now standing on the end of the leather couch and with an incredibly loud, retching sound, shot a geyser of green, acorn- studded vomit a good nine feet across the couch. It enveloped most of the living room, splattering over every piece of furniture and the area rug. A collective gasp/scream of horror was emitted by guests and hosts alike. "Oh. My. God!" said my daughter-in-law. Shy looked rather pleased with her work—she now felt better than she had before she had unloaded. For the dinner guests, however, it was a real conversation stopper.

The second of the memorable digestive incidents took place at our house. To this very day it is spoken of in hushed tones as "The Explosion." We will never know what caused it. We had been dog-sitting Shy while our kids were on vacation. The day before was uneventful. I had taken the three dogs in the woods for a hike and a swim. We had a normal dinner and so did they. Everybody was just fine. Or so we thought. We all went to bed and slept like babies. I am an early riser, so I was alone the next morning as I walked into the kitchen to let the dogs out. I was only half awake and totally unprepared for what awaited me.

As I neared the kitchen, an incredible, rank stench wafted towards me. I stopped in my tracks and told the dogs to stay, not wanting them to come into the kitchen till I saw what the source of the awful odor was. I have had dogs all my life, but never had I seen anything like this: The whole kitchen was splattered and covered in…well…there's just no nice way to say this…liquid poop. It was all over the floor, the cabinets, and the appliances. It had even splattered all over some CDs that had been left on the kitchen counters. The sheer volume of the mess was shocking.

I looked at the dogs—there were only two of them. My two boys were obediently staying where they had been told to, but very anxious to go out. Where was Shy? I found her in my room, hiding behind my bed. Dogs feel great shame if they have an accident in the house. It was very apparent from Shy's demeanor that she was the source of the kitchen massacre. I told her it was OK—she couldn't help it if she was sick. I woke up Bill, saying, "You are about to experience the worst wakeup call ever! Now get up and get the shop-vac as fast as you can…and don't go into the kitchen!"

I let the dogs out the front door to relieve themselves, and then rounded up rubber gloves and paper towels and disinfectant. By now, a grumbling Bill had come up the stairs with the shop vac. He looked in the kitchen he asked, "What the hell happened here?!?!"

"Poopageddon," I replied. As Bill surveyed the disaster area, he speculated on how Shy could have achieved this much…coverage. He came to the conclusion that she must have been spinning around like a lawn sprinkler shooting out liquid feces in all directions with a force that reached every nook and cranny in the kitchen.

I then explained to Bill that the way I saw the division of labor (and yes, participation was mandatory) was as follows: His division would go in with the heavy equipment, a.k.a. the shop-vac, and remove all the excrement that could be removed by the machine. Then he should take the vacuum outside and hose it. His phase of the operation would not require him to have his face or hands anywhere near the feces. I had learned from experience that this was the best Bill could do. Otherwise I would have two unspeakably horrible messes to clean up!

Then I would head in to do the hand cleaning. I knew I would have to be incredibly thorough, or I would never want to use the kitchen again. It was a very small kitchen, but it took over four hours to clean it to my satisfaction. When I was done, I was too exhausted to walk the dogs. They would have to play in the fenced-in yard today. I couldn't do another thing.

Bill came in from outside and told me he had started hosing the shop vac and had decided—since it was old and rusty and not a very expensive item, and since he never wanted to see it or, especially, never wanted to smell it again—that he would just throw it out. I told him I felt the same way about the whole kitchen…was that an option?

There was just no getting around it for her:
Shy had to learn to swim.

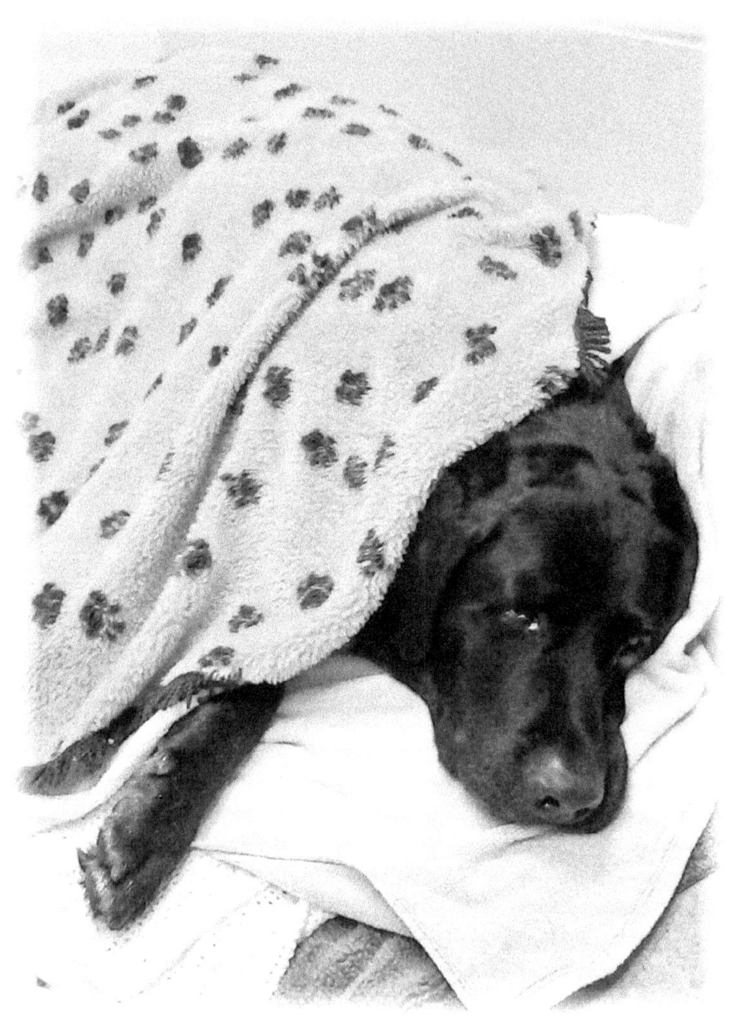

He was on several thicknesses of rugs,
covered by several layers of blankets.

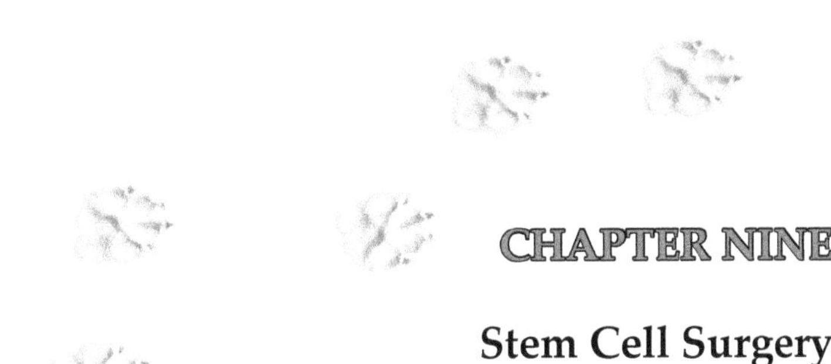

CHAPTER NINE:

Stem Cell Surgery: October 2012

Aging is not for sissies. And it is no different for our four-legged friends than it is for us. We had known for some time that Lakota had been born with joint problems, but his passion for running, jumping, and swimming, and his innate athletic talents had overcome and even hidden how bad his joints were. But there is only so much pain that can be ignored, and Lakota's pain was getting worse and worse. He still wanted to run and jump and play for all he was worth, but afterwards, he paid a terrible price. At night, when it was time to go out for the last time before bed, he could only walk very slowly, with great difficulty and pain.

Our vet had been trying different pain meds to give him relief, but they were irritating his digestive system. Lakota was eight years old and in great shape except for his elbow dysplasia and his arthritis. I couldn't bear to let him be in such pain, but his stomach couldn't tolerate the pain meds either. So I called made an appointment to talk to my vet about options. I was frightened because I was aware of the fact that arthritis was one of the most common reasons for euthanizing dogs. My vet answered the phone and when I told her of my fears, she asked if she could come by on her way home. She wanted to see how Lakota was functioning in his own home when he wasn't full of fear-based adrenaline at the vet's office. I was grateful that she was willing to do this.

When she came by, Lakota was on the floor and she sat down by him and started petting him and massaging him. As she massaged my dog and we talked, an odd thing happened; something that demonstrated how really well Lakota understood our language.

The town's fire alarm went off—a sound Lakota had heard for all of the years he had lived with me. He had never reacted to it, other than to show mild interest in the sound. Dr. Rao commented that when her dog heard the fire alarm, she would always put her head back and howl like a wolf. She did not howl herself or imitate her dog. She just spoke the words. But to our amazement, as soon as she finished her sentence, Lakota put his head back and howled a long, mournful howl. He had never done this for a fire alarm before and never did it ever again. It was as though he was saying, "I know exactly what you are talking about, because even though I don't speak your language, I do understand it." We all had a chuckle over the incident, and then I called Lakota and encouraged him to get up and move around the house for my vet to see.

Dr. Rao was very progressive and very proactive about keeping up on the latest innovations in veterinary medicine. She had something in her bag of tricks that was very new and bore a small risk, but had a shot at really helping Lakota: stem cell surgery. I listened intently as she told me about it.

Lakota would be put under anesthesia for the better part of a day. An incision would be made to remove fat from his shoulder area. That fat would be spun out in a centrifuge and processed and the stem cells would be removed from it. Those cells would then be injected into all of Lakota's joints and also run through his body in an I.V. If it worked, those cells would grow new cartilage to cushion his painful joints. It could give him relief for anywhere from one to five years.

The aftercare would be a challenge. Lakota could not run or jump—not even on furniture. He could only go up and down one or two stairs and very slowly. We had to keep him from jolting his joints even slightly to give the new cartilage time to harden. This had to be strictly followed for eight weeks or we would not have a good result.

The risks of the surgery were relatively low. The long anesthesia was one, but Lakota was strong and healthy and we weren't too concerned about that. There was no risk of rejection because the cells were his own. The one thing that did scare me was this: If there was an unknown cancer developing in Lakota's body, and if a stem cell became a cancer cell, the cancer would multiply rapidly. That was enough to give me second thought.

For the next few days, I pondered whether having the stem cell operation was the best for Lakota. As I watched him struggling to live his life in that painful body it became clear to me—even though he tried to hide it, as most dogs do—that he was suffering. The stem cell procedure was a shot at helping him, so how could I not take it?

Then, I got a helping push from right down the street. One of my neighbors told me about a girl who worked at our neighborhood deli who was raving about how much stem cell surgery had helped her arthritic dog. When I went to the deli to follow up on the information, the story was the same. The dog was going into its second year after the procedure and was still doing really well. I was ready to move forward.

We made the appointment for Lakota's surgery and set about turning our home into a customized doggy rehab center. I hope some readers will find the following information useful, because any kind of surgery has a recovery period and not all dogs will tolerate being crated. Since Lakota wasn't a crate dog and slept with me, we had to make the bed safe for him. Bill altered two dog ramps to make one long one so Lakota had an easy, not too steep way on and off the bed. We moved the bed towards the wall so the ramp was wedged between the bed and the wall, so it was impossible to jump off the side. For the other side of the bed, he made two stand-up wooden poles and attached temporary fence to them. The fence closed in my side of the bed like a crib so Lakota couldn't get off there. The bed was a sleigh bed with a high footboard, so he couldn't jump off the bottom of the bed either. If I needed to get up to use the bathroom, I would just roll up the fence, get out of bed, and roll it back to keep Lakota fenced in.

Then he made a wooden platform the length of the couch so Lakota could just step up onto and off of the couch with no jumping. Lakota was trained to keep off the other furniture and when he was trained to do something he was trustworthy, so that took care of the modifications inside the house. Since the back entrance had only two steps, we would just help him down with a lifting harness to keep his soft new joints safe. We had a ramp for the car and had the back of our small SUV set up with padding and pillows to keep him comfortable en route, and I was going to ride back there with him to keep him lying down the whole way.

After midnight on the night before the surgery, we had to fast Lakota and couldn't even give him water. I felt so guilty eating in front of him that I went down to the basement and grabbed a breakfast bar and a bottle of water so he didn't have to watch me and smell food. I didn't want to risk not eating, which could trigger a migraine. I needed to be fully functional today.

We dropped Lakota off at the vet's and went home to get some work done, since we knew he would be under anesthesia most of the day. When we arrived home and walked in, the house felt cold, quiet, and lonely without Lakota there. It was a palpable emptiness that I hadn't anticipated because it had been eight years since there was no dog in the house.

Around four-thirty that afternoon, my vet called me and said she wanted me to come over so I would be there when Lakota was coming out of the anesthesia. She said that dogs can hallucinate and become frightened when they are waking from a long anesthesia, and he would do better and be less anxious with me beside him, talking to him. It was precisely this kind of thing that made me a fan of Dr. Rao. I drove over to the vet's immediately—I couldn't wait to see my boy after a day without him. When I arrived I was taken into the back where Lakota was in a small room with a gate. He was on several thicknesses of rugs, covered by several layers of blankets. Dr. Rao told me that dogs shivered when they were coming out of anesthesia. It was normal, but she still liked to keep them warm with a lot of blankets. She opened the gate and brought me a chair to sit on while I stayed with Lakota. I talked to him and stayed close so he could get my scent. After a few minutes he started to cry softly, but as soon as I spoke reassuringly to him he stopped. It still was upsetting. Lakota was so stoic that I had not heard him cry since the incident with his front leg in the meadow.

Lakota had two rather large incisions. One was from the removal of a lipoma (benign fatty tumor) that we had asked the vet to remove while he was under anesthesia. The other incision was larger than I had anticipated and was from the fat extraction for the stem cells. The vet told me that they had a hard time getting enough fat for the stem cells because Lakota was muscular and didn't have much fat. That was the reason for the incision being larger than we had expected.

In a little while he started waking up. I sat on the floor and petted him and talked to him. He tried to get up a few times without success, and then finally made it to his feet. He was groggy and shaky, but clearly wanted to go home. The vet helped me put on his lifting harness and the vet tech picked up my eighty-two-pound dog and carried him out to the car.

When we got home, we drove on the lawn around to the back door where the entrance was just two steps. It took both of us to help Lakota out of the car and into the house. He barely made it in and collapsed in a heap, exhausted. I let him sleep right where he plopped down and stayed with him. We had been told that our dog would be wiped out for a few days. When an older dog is under anesthesia for the better part of a day, it does that. But we hadn't anticipated that he would be too weak to stand up and relieve himself. When it became apparent he didn't want to move, I brought him water and, later, a few very small amounts of bland food. And when it was time for bed, I slept next to him on an inflatable mattress.

When morning came and he still wouldn't go out, I called Dr. Rao. She said to give it some more time and call back if he didn't go by midafternoon. By early afternoon I was getting extremely anxious about it, so we put his lifting harness on and helped him out despite his reluctance. It became apparent that he wanted to go, but was too weak to hold himself in the position. We held him up and I kept asking him to "go pit stop," which was our term for this particular activity, and after much coaxing and pleading and even begging, he finally went. Then we helped our exhausted dog back into the house.

It was like this for two full days. On the third day, he was a little better. Never, at any time during his recovery period, did he ever refuse food. Lakota had an appetite that never quit! Once he was up and around, the problem became keeping him from jumping, running, or impact of any kind. The other issue was being sure that this dog—who had once eaten three and a half feet of vet wrap—left his drains and incisions alone.

To accomplish the latter, our vet had suggested putting a T-shirt on him. It is not easy to figure out what size T-shirt fits a dog. Before the surgery I had tried one of Bill's size extra-extra-large T-shirts on Lakota and it fit him beautifully, as long as I tied a knot on the top of his back, two-thirds of the way down towards the tail end. Because I would need to wash them frequently, I bought six new T-shirts for Bill and commandeered his six oldest ones to serve as Lakota's surgical dressings. It worked so well it was actually rather odd—sometimes the workings of a dog's brain are surprising. When I took off one of the shirts to change it, poor Lakota looked at his wounds and the drains and was terrified. His head drooped and his tail went between his legs and he looked downright shaky—almost like he might faint. As soon as I put the clean shirt on him his head and tail popped back up and he was "all better!!!!" As long as he couldn't see the wounds and the drains, to him they were gone.

We proceeded this way for the first week. He was allowed to walk the distance of two houses a day. This was rough for my boy, who was used to a one- to two-mile off-leash hike every day. But Lakota was a trooper and he handled it. I got him new toys and treat-dispensing games to play with, to help pass the time. Towards the end of the week I was leash-walking with him two houses down the street when a neighbor's loose dog charged at us, running towards us up the street. Normally, Lakota would have run out in front of me, guns blazing, and stopped that dog in its tracks. He was brave and fearless when it came to protecting me.

But he was full of stitches and had two big drains sticking out of him. He actually cried. I am neither brave nor fearless, but when I heard him cry, my maternal protective instinct kicked in. I knew that dogs were sensitive to energy—our intentions and the very essence of who we are project as our energy and dogs can read it well. So I stepped in front of Lakota, put my hand out, and said in my firmest voice, "STOP." I also shot a strong pushing/blocking thought out of my hand. The dog stopped so suddenly it was as if a rope had tightened around his neck. Clearly, the animal had gotten the message that I meant business. I firmly told it to go home, and to my amazement, it did. Since I suffer from anxiety, I don't have many brave moments. But moms—human moms or dog moms—are fierce!

The following day, I was less effective. We were walking in a different direction when a big woman with a large, horribly behaved dog came walking toward us. The dog was pulling and lunging closer and closer to us. I yelled to the woman that my dog had just had surgery and had stitches and drains and asked her to keep her dog away from us. But she had no control over this dog whatsoever, and the dog pulled her over to us and started jumping on Lakota. But now I was screaming at the woman and Lakota, wounded though he was, had no choice: He let out a roar like a lion, showed his teeth, and the other dog backed off.

I do not understand why people—so many of them—insist on having dogs they can't control. It's inconsiderate, stupid, dangerous, and unfair to others. But they are all over the place. The dog walker in our town says it's the biggest stress in her life. If you can't or won't have your dog trained, at least get a small dog you can handle when it's obnoxious. But that's not how it works. The woman with the dog she couldn't control, that jumped all over my injured dog, had no control over that dog, so (are you ready for this?)...she got a second one.

I looked Lakota over when we got home. Thankfully, he seemed none the worse for the wear. But for the life of me, I don't understand why people don't want to train their dogs. If you don't want to or don't have time to train a dog, get a cat...or a hamster...or a gerbil...or a bird. Or don't have a pet at all and give your neighbors and their animals a break.

In these video captures, Lakota tore out of the gate like the miniature quarter horse that he was. Cooper saw his buddy, free at last, and charged after him.

CHAPTER TEN:

The Big Reveal: October 2012

The eight weeks after Lakota's stem cell procedure went by more quickly than I had thought they would. Ten days after the surgery, we had to go to the vet's to have the drains and stitches removed. Dr. Rao was away, and her husband—also a vet and a co-surgeon on the project—was going to do the removal. I wanted to make this as un-traumatic for Lakota as possible, so I invoked the "power of the nose." Since scent is a dog's primary sense, I decided to make a bag of smelly, irresistible treats that would so engage Lakota's nose that he would hardly notice what was going on with his incisions. I cut up provolone cheese, cheddar cheese, liverwurst, and chicken into tiny pieces so I could just keep waving them in front of his nose, alternating the smells, and feed them to him. It worked surprisingly well, and he only turned around toward the vet once when one of the drains was being removed.

We kept up very limited but gradually increasing short walks on the leash for eight weeks, and I spent a lot of time with Lakota on mentally engaging tasks and games and slow, easy, obedience maneuvers. The measures we had put into place before the surgery to keep him from jumping on and off of the bed and the couch worked beautifully. On days when I felt Lakota getting bored or antsy, I took him for rides in the car or for very short walks but in new and different places. Dr. Rao had told me that the dogs she had operated on who had the best results were the ones who carefully followed the post-op restrictions, so I wasn't going to mess this up. The only doggy visitor we had allowed was Cooper, and we kept both dogs on a leash—even in the house—to keep them from breaking into one of their rambunctious games of chasing each other around the couch.

The procedure had been done in the fall but now it was transitioning into winter, and as the eighth week came and went, a fresh snowfall had accumulated about six inches of soft snow on the ground. The big day had come, at last, and now we would be able to see if our journey into somewhat uncharted waters had paid off. Of course, Elaine and Cooper had to be there for the big moment. Elaine and Cooper came up the street and stationed themselves at the bottom of the yard by the road. I brought Lakota out the back door. He seemed surprised that he wasn't on a leash. We walked to the gate, I opened it, and almost shouted, "OK—go ahead and run, run, run!"

Lakota tore out of the gate like the miniature quarter horse that he was. Cooper saw his buddy free, at last, and charged towards him. The two of them then went on the mother of all romps in the snow, running all around the yard, in and out of the open gate, sending sprays of white powder in every direction until I decided they'd had enough and called my dog in to rest. Phase one was complete. I had noticed that Lakota was running like a normal dog, using his back legs separately. Before the surgery he had run all the time with his back legs together—arthritis gait. He had never stopped running, but he would be crippled afterwards. The real test would be after his afternoon rest. Would he be able to get up? Would he be able to walk and go out? And what about tonight: Would he be able to get up for last out and walk?

We came in and had lunch. I went up to the loft office to get some work done and Lakota curled up for his afternoon nap. Around three p.m. I came down the ladder and held my breath. As I watched, Lakota stood up *quickly* and trotted over to me *like a perfectly normal dog!* He showed no evidence of pain at all and was eager for afternoon playtime. I teared up with joy, so happy that he wasn't suffering for his romp with his buddy. I called Dr. Rao to tell her the great news. The last test would be that night. Before his procedure, the last time going out at night had been the worst of the day. He had struggled to get up and it was clear how much pain he was in as he tried to move. If all went well, then this was a great success.

When the time came, I called Lakota to the door. He got up as though he didn't have a care in the world, trotted to me, then out the back door, down the two steps, and into the yard. I could hardly believe what I was seeing. This was a new frontier. It wasn't working for everyone, and we didn't know if it did work how long it would last. And there was the risk of accelerating an already present cancer if we were very unlucky. But here was my dog running around the yard looking very much like he wasn't in pain any more. If we hadn't done this, because of his stomach not being able to handle pain meds, we would not have been able to ease his terrible pain, and I would not have been able to watch him suffer. But this was a gift—a gift that had turned back the hands of time for us—and for however long it lasted, I was very grateful.

We started gradually getting back to our morning hike, increasing our distance a little each day. But it was like we were doing it for the first time, because I was watching my dog do it without pain. He was so joyful! And so was I. We took walks in the snow with Elaine and Cooper, and watched the two Labradors tear around the meadow in the snow, chasing each other like two puppies. And after a few weeks of this, I began to believe in it. I stopped being afraid, every morning, that I would wake up and we would be back to the way it was before the surgery. And we moved forward into a glorious, white winter, walking in magical, snowy, woods that looked like a scene from *Narnia*. It was the best of times.

Every morning, when we came back
from our walk, it was Lakota's job to go to the mailbox,
get the newspaper out of the newspaper box,
and carry it to the door and into the house.

CHAPTER ELEVEN:

Book Talk at the Senior Center: February 2013

It was a Saturday afternoon and I had a book talk scheduled at the senior center in a nearby town. The center had opened the talk to the public and they had a large room to host it, so we anticipated a large group. One of my girlfriends was coming along to help because we wanted to video record the event, and, as always, Lakota was to be the star of the show.

Until I started doing these events to promote *Walking with the Shadow of Love,* I had no idea how much my dog would be involved in the process. As it turned out, Lakota loved, loved, loved performing! He was the perfect warm-up act, and when his part of the program was finished, every person in the room was excited, engaged, and in love with Lakota. When I walked up to the podium I had an audience enthusiastically ready to hear "The Remarkable Story of Lakota and the Zeakie Dog." But what I couldn't anticipate was that on that day, Lakota was going to be involved in a way I never could have imagined.

Lakota was my rock. Nothing rattled him. He was so confident, calm, and able to handle almost any situation—with the possible exception of a trip to the vet—

that I could turn him loose in a room full of people while we were setting up. It didn't faze him at all that fifty-five strangers were touching him, talking to him, calling him, and even hugging him—something most dogs are very uncomfortable with. He loved people and he loved interacting with them. It didn't matter if they knew how to properly handle a dog, because nothing bothered him. He didn't mind his tail being held, being touched anywhere on his body, his food being moved or taken out of his mouth, his toys being taken, or anything else that might prompt another dog to growl or bite. So while we set up the cameras, the slide show, and the props for Lakota's part of the show, he just roamed free, greeted every person who came into the room, and walked around visiting everyone. I noticed that he went back to visit a distinguished looking, silver-haired man more than once, and that the last time he actually ran over to him in quite a hurry, but I didn't think anything of it.

Most people have not spent time around a highly evolved dog like this, and they are delighted. For these seniors, many of whom had dogs in the past but felt they couldn't handle one now, it reignited the joy of a close interaction with an animal, without having to worry they would be jumped on, knocked over, scratched, or any of the things that make seniors a little uncomfortable being around dogs who are not properly trained, calm, and polite.

When the time came to start, I called Lakota to me and introduced myself and Lakota, and started his portion of the show. I explained to the audience that many dogs loved to work, and that Lakota had a particularly strong work ethic. Truly, his favorite words were, "Help Mommy!" I went on to say that instead of teaching my dog cute tricks, I had taught him to do useful things, which gave him more satisfaction and gave me a helper.

Every morning, when we came back from our walk, it was Lakota's job to go to the mailbox, get the newspaper out of the newspaper box, and carry it to the door and into the house. This was actually helpful, because with hiking packs, water bottles, hiking poles, and the rest of our gear, we really didn't have a hand free for the paper. For our book talks, Bill had made a replica of our mailbox and we sent Lakota to it to fetch the newspaper, carry it to me, and drop it on cue. He did this with pure glee, and the audience loved it. As they applauded and I gave him a piece of cheese, he actually smiled!

Then I told him my feet hurt and asked him to get my slippers for me. This was a scene that frequently played out at home, although there I had to be careful. He liked to do this so much that if I accidently left my closet door open, he would bring every shoe I owned to me—a pair at a time. It was kind of like Mickey Mouse and the buckets of water in "The Sorcerer's Apprentice" section of Walt Disney's *Fantasia.* At the book talks he only had access to one pair of slippers that smelled like Mommy, and he carefully fit both of them in his mouth—not an easy feat—so he could bring them together, and brought them to me and dropped them at my feet.

Then I took him over to some bells that we had hung from a stand and gave him the "make music" command. He gleefully used his nose to make the loudest racket he could get out of them, delighting everyone watching. His joy and enthusiasm in doing these tasks was contagious, and the more appreciation he got from his audience, the more he loved doing it—he was a true doggy showman!

Last of all, I had him find a pair of gloves that I had dropped in the room. He sniffed around until he found them and trotted back with them in his mouth. His part of the show was now over, but that presented me with a problem.

The problem was that the warm-up act was so good that the main event could not possibly live up to it—Lakota upstaged me every time! So I learned to segue into my act by starting a slide show behind me, and tethering Lakota to me so he couldn't distract my audience from hearing my book talk. It worked well that way. The reason I know it did is that the woman who ran the senior center told me that it was the first time they ever had a program there where everybody was engaged so fully that they didn't have people sleeping! It had never occurred to me that this would be an issue with senior groups, but I got it—I've been known to drift off myself in front of the TV even if I'm watching something I like. But Lakota had the people here downright excited, and they were fully awake as I told them about the incredible journey I had taken with these two dogs, and how I now knew that animals had souls and went on in spirit form after they left here because I had been given the extraordinary blessing of witnessing it firsthand.

As I spoke I could see that some members of the audience were visibly moved, and I knew why. When I was five years old I went to church every Sunday with my parents. It was just something that was done and

I never questioned it—it was just normal…until one particular Sunday. On that day, the person conducting the service (I am not identifying the institution because it could have been any one of a number of religions preaching this at the time) was talking about animals. He said that they couldn't go to heaven because they didn't have souls. I literally gasped. Tears streamed down my face and I sobbed so loudly that my parents had to remove me and were clearly embarrassed. I, on the other hand, was devastated and angry. In my heart I knew it wasn't so, and in my heart—even though my parents made me continue to attend—I was done with this particular institution…at five years of age. I didn't throw the baby out with the bath water and I didn't lose my faith. I just lost faith in this particular church.

As I spoke to those seniors about the extraordinary event that had occurred when The Zeakie Dog left this world, also at only five years of age, I knew there were people in that room who had also been told, by religious institutions, similar things to what I had been told, when they were growing up. I also knew that there were people who had lost animals they loved deeply and were suffering the loss, wondering if their animals were just "gone" like they had been told they were. I was here to bear witness that their animals were not *gone*. I was here to bear witness that their animals did indeed have souls. And I was here to bear witness that their animals were around them at times, watching over them when needed, and blessing them with the same unconditional love they gave to them when they were here. Many, many people have had afterlife contacts from their animals—far too many for this to be a fluke of anyone's imagination.

Whenever I speak of this subject, I always want to be sure to address people who deeply love their animals and have *not* experienced any kind of contact. I had several dogs before the Zeakie Dog and Lakota that I also had very deep, loving bonds with. When they passed on it literally made me sick. When I lost my Labrador, Santana, I became so dangerously allergic to dogs that I couldn't have a dog for years. And yet, I never had any kind of spiritual contact from any of these dogs after they passed. I can only speculate as to why I didn't.

The first reason that occurs to me is that we have to be in the right state of mind to be able to receive these messages. Think of it as a radio that must be tuned in to receive a particular channel. At the time those dogs passed, I was living a very difficult, stressful life and was exhausted and sick most of the time. I had no time to meditate—something I do every day now--and was not in a state of mind to be observant. It could be that I was being sent contacts and was unaware.

The second reason that comes to mind is that, back then, I had no idea what form these contacts took. I had no idea what to expect, what to look for, how to be in the open and aware state to receive these gifts of spirit. Not that I am suggesting you should be constantly watching for such occurrences; they almost never happen when I am looking for them. They are always a surprise! The open and aware state comes in afterward, in recognizing them for what they are.

The third reason, which I mentioned in the Introduction, is that I believe some of us—those of us called empaths—are wired differently, neurologically. I have heard that a lot of us suffer from anxiety. Perhaps we have some sort of hyper-sensitivity in our brains that allows us to detect these types of connections.

My last theory as to why I can receive these contacts now, when I couldn't before, may surprise you, but it is what I believe is the truth. It is my opinion that—just as there are advanced souls among the human beings who walk this Earth—there are advanced souls among other species that we share this planet with. What happened as Zeak was leaving this world was initiated entirely by him and totally under his control. I believe that he was an advanced soul who was able to help me to open up my senses to be able to perceive things that I couldn't before. Just as there are some people who have very sensitive senses of smell and can detect scents that someone next to them may not be able to, I believe that this incredible dog had the ability to stimulate this energizing of my senses as he was leaving his physical body, so that we could keep in touch when he was no longer on this plane. I think I was almost there—he just had to give me a little push.

As I reached the end of my talk, I invited the audience to share any experiences they might have had that amounted to an awareness of their animals that had passed on being around them. I asked the audience to be open to the different forms that these contacts might take. But the first person who raised his hand to share a spiritual experience with an animal was not going to tell us about an incident with an animal who had passed on: He was about to recount something had had happened on this very day, in this very room, with my dog, Lakota, who was very much alive!

And I also knew the intense stare that the gentleman had described.

CHAPTER TWELVE:

Once a Therapy Dog, Always a Therapy Dog: February 2013

The man who raised his hand was the same silver-haired gentleman whom I had noticed Lakota going to visit more than once while we were setting up for the book talk. I also remembered that the last time I had seen my dog go to visit this man, Lakota had seemed to be in a hurry and actually broke into a trot to cross the large room to see the fellow. He was very distinguished looking, and what he had to say got everyone's attention.

Since it was a large room and I wanted everyone to hear what he had to say, I invited him up so he could use the microphone. He stepped up to the podium and addressed the audience, saying, "At the beginning of your talk, I had a spiritual experience with your dog." I was puzzled by this since Lakota was very much alive. The man then went on to say, "After I arrived here, your dog had come to say hello once or twice. I found a table, sat down, and just as I was getting settled I had an asthma attack. I fumbled in my pockets looking for my inhaler—I couldn't find it—and I could feel myself began to panic: If you've never had your breathing restricted, you have no idea how intense that anxiety is.

I found the inhaler and used it, but there is always a time lag before it starts working, and I was struggling to stay calm. All of a sudden your dog was there sitting in front of me, staring into my eyes intensely. He locked in on them—it was almost as if he was hypnotizing me—I could actually feel him calming me down and my chest relaxing! This really happened and I wanted you and everyone here to know."

A silence hung over the room as people absorbed what the silver-haired man had shared. I thanked him and stepped back to the podium. I told the audience that what the gentleman had shared did not surprise me one bit. The reason for this was that I had asthma too, so Lakota was well versed on asthma attacks and the panic that goes with them. Dogs can detect seizures before they happen, rising blood sugar levels, and they can even smell cancer in human saliva. So it was no surprise that Lakota knew how to handle an asthma attack. And I also knew the intense stare that the gentleman had described. That stare was how Zeak began the remarkable event that occurred as he was dying. And, oddly enough, since Zeak's departure, Lakota had started doing this to me every night around seven-thirty p.m., as I was relaxing in my chair watching TV in the living room. He was relentless and the stare was so intense that I couldn't ignore it or concentrate on my shows. What I think he wanted was for me to go to bed with him, but I didn't want to go to bed so early. I never had, and I had no idea why he wanted me to. I also noticed something I had seen with Zeak's eyes at the beginning of the occurrence when he was dying: As Lakota kept staring his eyes were getting lighter—almost translucent. What I believe now is that Lakota's spirit was getting stronger and his body was getting weaker: Some process had begun that was going to end his life. But at this early stage I had no clue anything was wrong—he appeared to be in robust good health.

The next person to speak was a woman who was visiting from Germany. She told us that she'd had occurrences like this happen with her cats over her whole life, but had never told anyone because she was afraid they would think she was crazy. She had no idea that other people were having similar incidents, and she said that now she would be more comfortable talking about what she had experienced.

Another woman raised her hand to speak. She said that she had been watching Lakota while I was speaking, and that he was sleeping beside me until I started talking about Zeak. When I started talking about Zeak, she had noticed that Lakota woke up and started following something around the room with his eyes. No one was moving around the room. She was convinced that he was looking for Zeak. I added that if he was following something around the room like that, he was probably seeing Zeak. I had seen it many times at home, and I was convinced that not only could he see him, but he could smell him, too, because as he was following the apparition around the room, he was also occasionally lifting his nose and air-scenting.

Another woman shared with us that she had a cat she thought was seeing spirits in her home. Twice every evening her cat would get up from wherever she was sleeping, walk to the bottom of the stairs, and stare at something that she suspected was moving down the steps in her living room. She could not see a thing, but her cat could, and this went on twice every evening for years.

The last person who had a story to tell was a middle-aged woman who had lost her dog about six months earlier. The dog had a natural passing at home, by the kitchen door. The woman said that when the dog left its body, she saw a clear, transparent form rise up and go out the door.

So many people have had these experiences. It's just not reasonable to think that all of us, who are perfectly functional human beings in every other way, are out of our minds in just this one specific way. There are many more of us than anyone knows about, because most of us are afraid to speak up about our experiences, fearing judgmental comments from the scientific community. I don't understand how they can be so sure of their point of view, when they reverse their "absolute scientific truths" on everything so frequently—for example, last year coffee was bad for us. This year coffee is good for us. Next year it will be bad for us again. They dismiss anything they can't explain in a way that often involves disparaging the people who have personally had these experiences.

I personally had to deal with this bias when I developed fibromyalgia syndrome. The medical community didn't understand it, so they labeled it a psychological issue. Then they decided it was "real" and classified it as a nerve disorder. And recently they are considering it to be a "post-viral syndrome." Meanwhile, those of us needing help are mislabeled and misled. Everyone makes mistakes, but when you are doing real damage to the people you should be helping, you should hold back on judgments when you don't really know.

Another example of this is the medical community's opinions on tuberculosis in the past century. At one time, they were sure that it was a psychiatric disorder. When the bacteria responsible for the disease was finally discovered, many doctors refused to believe it—even though there was clear evidence of the bacteria—and still insisted that the disease was psychiatric. Imagine the harm they did to people suffering this terrible illness, going to their doctors for help and being called "crazy."

The moment I saw her,

I knew she was coming home with us.

CHAPTER THIRTEEN:

Izzy: August 24, 2016

I have a blog on the *Walking with the Shadow of Love* website. In August of 2016, a response to my blog was posted. It told the story of a cat named Izzy. It touched my heart, because the cat and its owner waged the same battle, with the same enemy, as Zeak and I did. The cat was even also four years old when it was stricken with lymphoma. Izzy and her humans walked the same path with the same vet. The love the owner of this cat had for her pet was palpable. The post was so beautifully written that I decided to include it in this book, in its original form as written by "Samantha."

On October 29, 2010, my husband and I walked into our local animal shelter to look for our next family member. Not quite ready for a human of our own, we felt that a cat would be a great start. We scoped out every cage and living area, and wound up in the "cat room," where about forty cats spent their days together.

It was Heaven. Every cat knew how to play the "adopt me" game. I was covered in cats, each one showering me with attention, in the hopes that their pageantry would win them a ticket out. I wanted to adopt them all. And then, I turned and scanned the room.

There she was. Sitting upright on a bench, waiting patiently for me to notice her. A gorgeous brown and black tabby with beautiful, soulful, trusting green eyes. The moment I saw her, I knew she was coming home with us. I tilted my head and said "Hello" and she inspected me with some sniffs as I knelt to be on her level. Then she turned to look at my husband, who was waiting patiently by a cat tower, largely ignored. She jumped down, traversed the room, and marched on top of the tower to inspect him too.

We went to dinner after our shelter visit and talked about the cat we wanted; she was the clear choice. The next day, on Mischief Night, we signed the papers and took Izzy home. After a few hours of hiding in her new home, we heard her emerge from her safe spot and ask, "MrrrrrrRRRRH?"

Every mom thinks her baby is special, and I was no exception. Except, she truly was. Our connection with Izzy was so powerful, and she made our family complete. We talked to each other (the sounds that came out of her mouth were unbelievably conversational). She never complained, and never hissed a day in her life. She greeted me at the door when I returned from work. She slept on my husband's arm. She fought the hair dryer, her archenemy. We came home from vacations early just to be with her because we missed her so much. We just loved her, and she loved us. Everything was perfect.

And then, she sneezed blood.

*Respiratory infection? Fungal infection? Benign polyp? There was no chance in hell that our robust, healthy, vibrant four-year-old had f***ing cancer. And we treated her for everything else for over a month. Izzy's nose was growing this mass, this ugly, ever-changing, brownish-pinkish-whitish mass. I watched it grow. I watched it change hourly. I took* *photos and examined them like I knew what I was looking for. All I knew was that there was no-way-by-the-grace-of-God that THIS was happening.*

But it was.

The phone call came that night.

Lymphoma. It was the best of the worst news. It's the most highly treatable form of cancer. Treatable doesn't mean curable. There are no real options. We're sorry.

My baby was dying.

*I had thought ahead and made an appointment with a veterinary oncologist earlier that week so if I got s***ty news, I could act faster. Our appointment was on September 15th, World Lymphoma Awareness Day.*

We were presented an à la carte menu of three options. Say Your Goodbyes Now, A Little More Time, or Maybe She'll Make It if You're Lucky. We chose the longest running option and our best chance to make a difference.

Fast-forward through the next four and a half months, where we declined every family invite and any chance to leave our apartment, outside of work. Our lives became consumed with finding alternate remedies, shuffling Izzy to chemotherapy, and trying to find something, anything, that would cure her. Even as we watched her beautiful, long whiskers fall out one by one, we still thought we would be that success story, touting a healthy cat eight years out. We wanted her to be happy and pain-free.

It became clear right after the New Year passed, after we learned that the cancer had spread to Izzy's kidneys, that there wasn't much time left with her. We gave her the last possible chemotherapy treatment and stopped all functioning and contact with the outside world, except to field possible end-of-life options.

We chose a fantastic veterinarian to come to our home to help her pass when the time was "right," whatever that means. I mean, the time was far from "right." Izzy just celebrated her fifth birthday in August. However, she deserved to depart in her favorite spot, not some office that she was terrified to go to. We owed her that.

Izzy passed away in our home on January 22, 2015. The morning was so cloudy that I didn't think she'd get her sunbeam to lay in. However, in the same moment that the fatal dose of anesthesia was administered, and her chest rose and fell for the last time, a sunbeam flashed so brightly in her spot and was gone in an instant.

It was her. It was my baby leaving this world and jumping into the spirit world. It had to be her. Nothing else would have been so bright.

In the days that followed Izzy's passing, I begged and pleaded for her to give me a sign that she was all right. I saw her in the clouds and heard her in my mind, but it didn't seem quite real until I felt her.

Izzy used to climb onto the bed every morning before I woke up and make a place for herself on my right side for the sole purpose of getting belly rubs. We would lay there together while it was still dark outside, me hearing her soft purr when I placed my head on her chest. She truly was the best alarm clock ever.

One morning, as I lay in bed curled up in the comforter, I reached out to find Izzy like I had done so many times. As my hand scanned the sheet, I found a warm spot. An impossibly warm spot. A spot that had faint heat despite the fact that I wasn't laying there previously. I knew she was there and was comforting me. She knew how badly I wanted to rewind time and just hold her again.

Weeks passed before I felt her again.

One morning, after I got out of the shower, I headed into the bedroom to get dressed. As I reached the dresser on my side of the bed, the dresser that Izzy would stare at intently, waiting for me to throw one of the ten tinfoil balls I had stashed in there at any given time, I felt heat again.

It was like a warm breeze. The feeling was unmistakable. It first touched my left calf and then my right. It was gone as fast as it came. It was my little girl. I can tell now when she lets me know she's around. She was rubbing against my legs.

I should have thrown a ball.

Spirits can contact us via any of our senses. Samantha's cat reached her through the sensations of touch. I have had spirits come to me in four different senses that I am aware of. On numerous occasions, I have clearly seen Lakota and I have seen Zeak as a shadow. I both saw and heard my mother after she passed. I smelled my father's cherry tobacco pipe smoke in the bathroom at three a.m. on the night after his funeral. (We have a smoke-free home.) I also smelled my aunt's powerful (and awful) perfume that gave me migraines out on my porch after she passed. But now it didn't give me a headache. I have felt Lakota pressed up against me in bed and felt Zeak rub against my leg on more than one occasion. The only sense I have not felt spirit contact with is taste. However, I have heard of others experiencing taste sensations related to spiritual contacts. Everyone is different in this regard. One of my friends receives most of her pet contacts through hearing: clairaudience. I tend to have more visual contacts: clairvoyance.

The second visit Lakota and I were doing that week was a home visit.

CHAPTER FOURTEEN:

Job Fatigue: April 2013

We had two therapy dog visits on the calendar this week. The first was to a lovely, assisted living facility about fifteen minutes away, and Elaine and Cooper were going with us. We enjoyed the scenic drive, chatted along the way, and pulled into the circular driveway right on time. Visiting with therapy dogs is not without some risk. One has to be concerned about the transmission of infections in many directions: from patient to dog, from dog to patient, and patient to handler. And chemicals used in cleaning can be dangerous to dogs. However, this time the issues began the minute we got out of the car.

We could see that gardening was being done at the facility. We had to let the dogs relieve themselves before taking them into the building, but we had to be concerned about whether or not pesticides, herbicides, chemical fertilizers, grub controls, or other toxic materials dangerous to our dogs had been used on the lawns or landscaping. Since we couldn't find anyone to ask, we directed the dogs to go in a patch of woods nearby. As we pondered the unseen dangers in the modern world, my thoughts went to a trip to a former vet's office with Lakota, years back.

This particular vet was always very busy and running late. As we sat in the waiting room, a young man came in with a beautiful but frail-looking yellow Labrador puppy and sat next to us. Before I let the dogs say hello, I asked if the pup had anything contagious and the owner indicated that he did not. I told him Lakota was there for a vaccine and was not contagious, either. Lakota loved puppies and the two dogs hit it off and were passing the long wait enjoying each other, while the pup's owner and I chatted. What he had to tell me was shocking and made me vigilant ever after about the issues that had caused his dog to be there.

The young man and his wife lived in a condo community nearby. Their Labrador pup was eighteen months old. My jaw dropped when the man told me they were here at the vet's because the puppy was dying of kidney disease at this young age. My mind immediately went to a recent dog food recall that had resulted in canine deaths from kidney failure, but it was not food that was doing this beautiful young puppy in. It was his daily walk.

Every day the puppy's owners dutifully and joyfully took a nice long walk with their dog twice—in the morning and after dinner. The community they lived in had beautiful grounds and walking paths and it was a part of their day that they really looked forward to unless the weather was awful. If it was, they still did it...but minus the joy. It never one occurred to them that these lovely walks could be killing their dog.

The dog started developing symptoms of illness and they took it to the vet to be checked out. By the time they figured out what was going on, the dog was in the throes of renal failure. Evidently, the well- manicured grounds of their condo were kept that way by heavy use of chemical poisons. Every day after their puppy's walk, they went to work and he stayed home and… licked his paws. What he didn't ingest by licking off, he absorbed through his feet. He was too far gone to save. All they could hope for was to keep him as comfortable as possible for a little longer until his quality of life was too poor to maintain.

People who are isolated from nature in the cities, or those who have hectic, busy schedules, exercise in gyms, and don't have time to interact with nature or be outdoors, are insulated from seeing how toxic our planet is becoming to life of all kinds…including our own. When people hear that one-third of dogs will get cancer and one-half of dogs over ten will get cancer, they are surprised. I don't use anything on my lawn but organics that can literally be eaten. My lawn isn't perfect and has clover and some weeds in it. But my dogs' health has always been more important. Hearing about this puppy dying from lawn chemicals just broke my heart. How do people in communal living know where it is safe to walk their dogs? In our state, flags are supposed to be put out to warn people of chemical use, but few do it and there is no one to enforce it. Let the dog walker beware.

And so, Elaine and I did our best to avoid any such hazards and entered the facility where our boys were about to do their job. As we approached the front desk, several residents approached us wanting to see the dogs. I told them we would be right with them, but we had to sign in first. We signed the facility's book and the receptionist signed our sheet to document our visit. Then we started to circulate.

The seniors were always delighted to see the dogs, and because Lakota and Cooper were both black Labradors, we were inevitably asked if they were related. "They're not related, but they're as close as brothers," I always answered. "Brothers from another mother," Elaine liked to say. And it was the truth. The two big dogs were petted, talked to, loved on, and moved from person to person, totally aware that was what they were here for. We finished seeing everyone on the first floor and the receptionist asked us if we would visit "The Villa," which was their name for the dementia/ Alzheimer's section.

We walked down a long hallway, and then we had to do my least favorite thing: get on an elevator. I am claustrophobic, and elevators are very stressful and difficult for me. I was glad Elaine was with me, and Lakota did his therapy dog work for his Mommy on the elevator. It was only one floor up, but for me it was an endless ride. The doors couldn't open fast enough to make me happy, and I breathed a sigh of relief when we got off.

This facility had a wonderful staff who worked hard at keeping the residents engaged. That was difficult with this group of people, and the caretakers were always delighted to see us, because the dogs were able to pull many of the dementia/Alzheimer's patients out of their trancelike states and get them to interact. We worked our way around the room and visited each and every person, and then I had Lakota do a few tricks for the group. The tricks were less engaging with this group than they were with the more mentally functional group downstairs. This group needed one-on-one contact. We stayed a while and also visited with the staff. The workers at these facilities were doing very stressful, demanding jobs, and we were there for them too. It really brightened their day to see the dogs, so we were always sure to interact with them as well.

Lakota always let me know when he had enough. Therapy dogs absorb the stress of the people they are visiting and should not work more than about ninety minutes. This varies from dog to dog, and is also dependent on whom they are visiting. My experience has been that seniors are more draining on the dogs' energy than children are, even though the children are usually more excited. It is very important for a handler to know when their dog has had enough, and not make the dog work beyond that point. With Lakota, it was easy. He always let me know by making eye contact and producing a little whining sound. He never whined other than under these circumstances: It was his way of communicating that he had done all he could. We exited the facility and took the dogs to the park for a short walk on the trail before going home.

The second visit Lakota and I were doing that week was a home visit. A woman I had worked with when I was teaching had heard I had a therapy dog, and asked if I would bring Lakota to visit her husband, who was battling a debilitating lung disease. They lived in a lovely fifty-five-and-up community about twenty minutes from our home. When we got there, there was another elevator involved. I didn't want to deal with it, so Lakota and I took the stairs. It was good exercise and going up was not hard for my boy. Going down I would need to take the elevator, though, because that was difficult for him.

We entered my former coworker's lovely home and she greeted us warmly. I had always enjoyed her and it was good to see her again, but sad to see her husband struggling with his illness. He had been a very successful man in a high-level position who was deeply loved by his family, and it was hard to see him so compromised by this illness. He seemed in good spirits during the visit, and Lakota sat with him for about half an hour, while the man petted him and just enjoyed the company of a nice, calm dog. He asked if we could come back sometime and I told him we would be happy to.

When we visited him the next time, his illness had taken a toll. We were there for a shorter amount of time and it was clear that he was not doing well. Even though he was on oxygen, his lips had a blue tinge and he seemed weaker. He was only up to a short visit, and then we departed. That was the last time we saw him. He passed soon after that, and it was devastating to his family to lose such a great man. With a mutual friend, I met his wife—my former coworker—for lunch, a while later. She told me that shortly after his passing, one evening, a picture of her that had hung on their wall for many years suddenly, and for no apparent reason, just fell off the wall. She wondered if her husband was letting her know that he was around. I told her that considering the experiences I had had over the last few years, I thought that was a good guess.

I do believe our loved ones, human and animal, try to let us know they are still around. Being separated from those we love is excruciating, and I know they try to help us. Many times we miss the signs. We just don't connect a flickering of lights or finding a feather where there should not be one to a loved one's presence. A butterfly landing on us and behaving strangely is seen as a random event because we don't notice that it is happening on a date connected to someone who has crossed over. Or a song of significance comes on the radio on the anniversary of a loved one's passing, but we don't recognize this because we are distracted.

I had suffered many losses before The Zeakie Dog opened me up to being able to detect these occurrences. I had lost both people and dogs that I loved, but I never detected them around me. It was as if I had the wiring, but the power had never been turned on. The profound spiritual experience I had when Zeak passed awakened that ability in me. It was as though he wasn't going to leave without giving me a way to stay in touch. So even though some of us may be born empaths, we may need a push to function as such.

I also believe that certain souls are better at certain kinds of contacts. Just as we have talents here, we have talents after we cross over. The Zeakie Dog has visited me many ways, some of which have taken my breath away. But while I have seen his form as a shadow and seen him in a dream visit, at this point in time, I had never had a full, solid, detailed visualization of him. Yet, many people have had those kinds of visits from departed loved ones. At any rate, I had been dazzled by so many thrilling, unexpected contacts from Zeakie that, while I delighted in every one, I was beginning to take them in stride. That is, until something happened—I don't know how, who, or why—that knocked me off my feet...and in a good way!

So we took the plunge.

Never for even a moment did we regret it.

CHAPTER FIFTEEN:

The Gift: June 2013

Years back, when The Zeakie Dog had been diagnosed with terminal cancer at age four, we were not prepared for it. We were not prepared emotionally, physically, or financially. We had taken out health insurance for both of our dogs to help prepare for unforeseen illness, but we had no clue what treating a dog for cancer could cost.

Those of you who have read *Walking with the Shadow of Love* know that our vet at that time called with the diagnosis: stage 4 a/b lymphoma. That is a point on the cancer rating scale that tells us that the cancer has advanced, and in this case has spread to the liver and spleen, and the dog is feeling well in some ways and not in others. The vet said that Stage 5 was the end and told us our four-year-old dog could be gone in a few days if we didn't act immediately. We had no time to think about it. He said the only thing that could buy Zeak some time was chemotherapy. He also told us that dogs tolerated it very comfortably. They were given only enough to slow down the disease, because trying to cure it with high doses like they give to humans would be unethical, since the dog could not have signed on for the accompanying misery. And if we were lucky and got a remission Zeak could feel perfectly normal for an extended period of time…a year or more. Proportionally, life-span wise, that would be like giving a human roughly eight more years at a high quality of life.

So we headed to Dr. Seiford, the veterinary oncologist he sent us to. And we were blessed with a remission—against all odds for a number of reasons—due to Dr. Seiford's skill and dedication. I thought our insurance would cover most of the treatment. It had a cap of $12,000 for an illness. It never occurred to me that keeping my dog alive and well could cost somewhere in the neighborhood of buying a new car!

Both of our vehicles were old with high mileage, but were in good shape. We had been thinking of replacing one, but decided to keep it going and get the missing funds from our home equity. We knew we could manage the payments—it would just mean we would have them for a longer period of time than we did now. We both felt it was worth it. We didn't hesitate to do this for this incredible dog because he was only four years old and deserved the best we could give him. We also did it because he was so ill that the only other choice was to put him down. His head was swollen up like a soccer ball and he was too weak to go for even short walks. And he was nauseous and losing his appetite. The treatments would make him feel well again.

This had all happened so quickly it was hard to grasp. Before that he was a happy, active dog. If he had been an old dog we probably would not have plunged into waging this very costly war with cancer.

So we took the plunge. Never for even a moment did we ever regret it. After Zeak left the physical world, we were comforted that we had given him the best, longest life that we could possibly give him. And as time passed, we managed to pay our bills and our cars kept on running for us. But we were getting on in years and finances were getting tight. Just as I was really starting to stress over the situation, one day, out of the blue, an unexpected letter came in the mail. It was from one of Bill's old employers...a previous owner of the company he used to work for. When he opened the envelope I saw shock on his face. The letter informed him that he had a retirement account that had not been rolled over when the new owners took over. The amount of money in the account was exactly enough to pay off all of Zeakie's remaining bills plus the remaining balance on the home equity account!

We both had to sit down. We had never won anything more than a couple of bucks on a lottery ticket. We had both worked for many years for what we had. And it's not like we hadn't been short on funds before. This kind of thing just didn't happen to us...but it had! Tears of joy and gratitude rolled down my face, and I said a prayer thanksgiving. A huge burden had been lifted from us.

I believe that after we pass on, we continue in spirit form and all become a part of God...akin to how each molecule that makes up our body is a part of us. Once that happens, every spirit is a part of an all-knowing being and has full awareness of the goings-on down here. So, I had no idea whose blessing this incredible gift was. I just extended thanks to all who might have participated in it, and the list of names and spiritual beings was long! In the end, I believe it all comes from one unified source, but God chooses to connect with us in many different ways...the ways we can best receive his love and guidance. That is why I have a lot of tolerance and respect for other religions. I have no desire to change anyone else's views. This is just what my life has taught me. And while some may not believe this, I knew in my heart that The Zeakie Dog had at least some part in this because the way he departed from this Earth was the sign of a highly evolved spirit.

As I pondered this blessing we had received, I was moved to reflect on questions of spirituality. I have always hesitated to use—in the presence of others--the sentence, "My prayers were answered," for a number of reasons. This is not to say that I don't express gratitude when I feel my prayer requests have been granted. It is more out of respect for others who are worthy—perhaps far more than I am—and have had tragic things happen to them, where they have prayed for a positive outcome, but it has not happened. Why do some people get miracles and some people get clobbered? I have seen some of the best, kindest, people I know suffer what seems like great injustices and some of the worst people I know seem to always get their prayers answered. This subject has been the subject of much thought. Much has been written on the subject, such as the story of Job in the Bible, or the book titled, *When Bad Things Happen to Good People,* by Harold S. Kushner. I believe all prayers are heard and answered, but sometimes the answer is no. Some of us are so blessed and others suffer, but there seems to be no correlation in this to the quality of the human being involved. I deeply admire those whose faith is tested when they endure a tragic loss and their prayer requests are not granted. Especially when they maintain trust in their higher power and keep their faith, accepting that there must be a higher purpose that is the reason their prayers were not answered in the way they so hoped they would be.

A couple of months after our manna from heaven arrived, Bill got some bad news: The company that he had worked at for thirty-four years was downsizing and his job was being phased out. He would get a severance package, but it was too soon for him to collect social security. If it had not been for "the gift" paying off our home equity loan, we could have been in serious trouble. Someone was really watching our backs. This allowed Bill to retire without duress and we were able to limp along on his severance pay until he was able to collect social security. It was also a blessing for me, because I was struggling to run the house, do the grocery shopping, take care of Lakota, and also do some therapy dog visits when I felt up to it, while dealing with the limitations of my health issues. I was exhausted a lot of the time. It would make life easier and more enjoyable for me to have some help.

I had seen a few of my friends' husbands have a very hard time retiring. Some got depressed. One spent many months just sitting on the couch. I decided that was not going to happen in our household if I could help it. So I encouraged Bill—strongly—to join us on our morning hikes. It would be safer for us to have another adult along to discourage bears and coyotes from approaching us, give Bill some exercise, and hopefully, help prevent a case of the post-retirement blues. I was especially concerned about the effect of retirement on Bill because he had not initiated the retirement himself.

He agreed it was a good idea, so he started to join us on our adventures in the woods. It gave him an opportunity to see Lakota do his athletic charging around the woods and into the lake. It was a beautiful sight to see this dog in his element. It was an opportunity to commune with nature—which I believe is good for all of us—and enjoy taking some photographs. Fortunately, Bill got into it and is still doing it with us as of this writing.

We took Lakota hiking on the trails every day that the weather allowed. Most days Elaine and Cooper joined us. Sometimes other neighbors joined us with their dogs. Sometimes our granddog Shy was visiting and would come along. The dogs had a blast and got plenty of exercise, enabling them to stay in good shape. And the walks also helped us to stay healthier and mobile. This is something we need to be concerned about as we age. Staying fit doesn't just happen automatically—you have to work at it just to keep from losing ground. With the health issues I had, I barely made it through my days. Working outside the home was out of the question. Bill might have been able to, but I had been struggling to keep up, and with him at home it got easier for me. This allowed me to do some things I very much wanted to do: my artwork and writing. These things would never have been possible without "the gift."

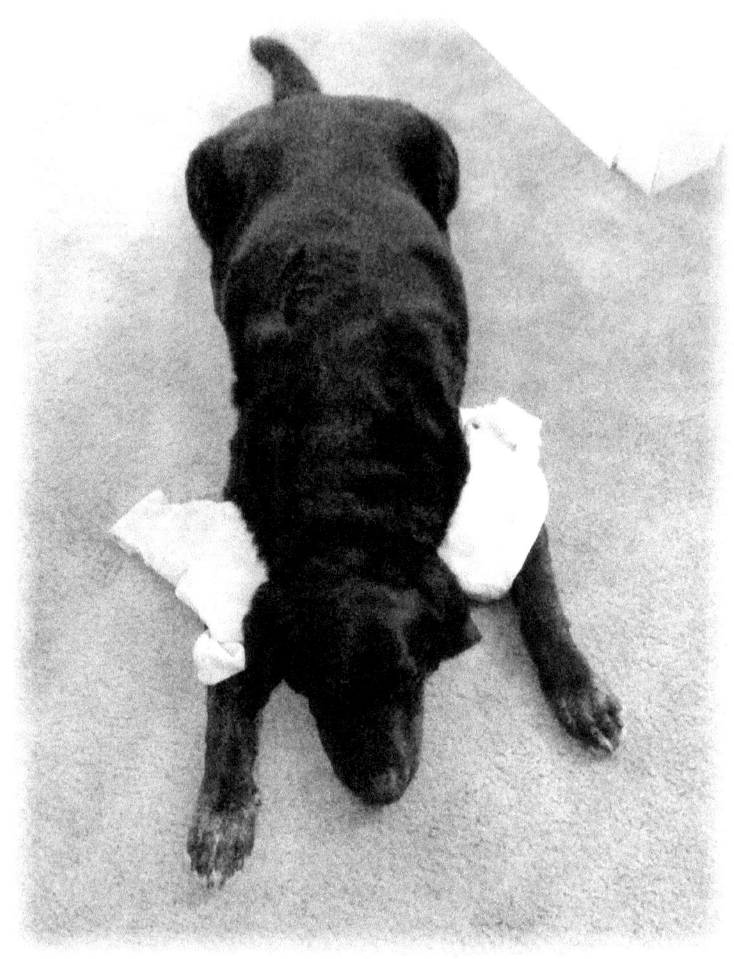

Lakota was a cooperative patient.
He allowed me to ice the areas that needed it.

CHAPTER SIXTEEN:

Age Appropriate? November 2015

My friend Vicki lives in a rural area about forty-five minutes to the north and west of our home. Her house is on a large lot, part of which is cleared and part wooded. Her home is built up about three feet from the surrounding ground, and the land around the house is stabilized by stone walls. She has such a large yard; a lot of her friends like to visit for play dates with her dogs. Because it is so rural, and set back so far from the road, the dogs could play off leash, and it was the site of many romps of epic proportions.

On this particular afternoon late in the fall, one of the neighbors was watching their parents' dogs for them while they were away. The dogs had all been around each other before, so they knew each other and it was no problem for these dogs to join the romp. But there was an issue involved in the addition of the extra dogs.

One of the dogs was a lovely, sweet Labrador Retriever who sadly had bad hips, but still got around pretty well. The other was an equally nice dog—a Cockapoo, which is a mix of Cocker Spaniel and Poodle—and therein was the problem. The problem had nothing to do with any fault of the dog. In fact, the problem was quite the opposite.

In the world of humans there are certain beings endowed with great beauty, combined with some sort of animal magnetism, and good fortune. This trio of qualities sometimes results in the emergence of a mega star. Marilyn Monroe, Elizabeth Taylor, Sophia Loren, Brigitte Bardot, Halle Berry, and Jennifer Lopez are a few that come to mind. They are put on pedestals and have throngs of cult-like fan/worshippers who adore them and will go to any lengths, pay huge amounts of money, and travel great distances to get a mere glimpse of them. But until this particular late fall day, I had no idea this existed in the dog kingdom. But it evidently does, and in this case it was in the form of a Cockapoo named Lady.

For some reason, all of the dogs l-o-v-e-d Lady. They all wanted to be near her, play with her, chase her, and have her attention. And my old boy, Lakota, was no exception. If he were a human, he would have been wining and dining her, buying her expensive gifts, and standing out in the rain serenading her to win her heart. Evidently, the dog version of this involved showing off for her by ignoring your aging body, chasing her around for all you were worth, and running faster and harder than any of the other dogs could. At this point in time, Lakota was two months from his eleventh birthday. He was at an age where most Labs are arthritic and geriatric and not running so fast and hard any more—if they are running at all. Some may even have trouble walking. Some have not even made it this far.

But Lakota had always been a very athletic dog, and when arthritis caught up with him a few years back—as noted in an earlier chapter—we had him stem-celled with great success. So our boy could still run around with his younger friends and give many of them a run for their money. He was all muscle and in great shape, so I never stopped him from participating in these romps because it was his joy and his pleasure. And since his stem cell procedure, he had been able to do it with no soreness afterwards. But on this day, I failed to factor in the fact that Lakota was madly, passionately, even blindly mad about Lady.

Lakota began pursuing Lady with a zeal beyond the age limitations of his body. One whiff of her intoxicating doggie aroma and he was transformed into a combination of Joe DiMaggio, John F. Kennedy, and Robert F. Kennedy, all in hot pursuit of Marilyn Monroe—regardless of the consequences. Round and round the large yard Lady tore at top speed—she was only three years old and also in great shape—with Lakota in hot pursuit, and the rest of the dogs trailing behind. It went on for a long enough time that a couple of the dogs dropped out, exhausted, but not Lady and not Lakota. At this point I was getting ready to stop it, because I didn't want Lakota to overdo it, and it was apparent that he was out-of-his-mind determined to catch the flying Cockapoo. But—as has happened before in my life—while my instincts were correct, they were about two seconds too late.

As I mentioned at the beginning of this chapter, there was a wall that raised the land all around the house. It was about three feet high and ended on grass, so it normally wouldn't be a problem jump for most dogs to make. Until now, the dogs had avoided it, but the Cockapoo couldn't shake Lakota, so she was now going to do some evasive maneuvers to see if she could shake her over-ardent fan. She ran up the stairs in the wall to the higher ground around the house; then she headed straight for the wall at full speed and jumped off of it, going so fast that she became airborne. This was no problem—for her. She was a smaller, lighter, three-year-old dog. But for my much larger, heavier Labrador who was running at full throttle, it was like a locomotive barreling off a three-foot wall. And the results were equally disastrous.

Lakota landed from his jump, but that was where all action stopped. He was very stoic and uttered not a peep, so as not to embarrass himself in front of his hottie gal pal, but he was hurt. So hurt that we could barely get him home. He completely avoided putting one front leg down and it was clearly very painful to put weight on the other one. I put his car harness on him because it was heavily padded and would allow me to help lift the weight of his front legs without cutting into him. I couldn't lift my boy myself, so I sent for reinforcements, and Vicki's husband came over to help. I took Lakota home and settled him down with some ice packs. It was too late for my vet to be open, so I would have to wait for the next morning to have him checked out and see exactly what his injuries were.

Getting Lakota to the vet the next day was not easy. He could not put any weight on one of his front legs, and the other was so painful he didn't want to. We got him in and out of the SUV by using his car harness as a lifting harness. Then we did the same to get him from the vehicle into the vet's office, one slow, painful step at a time. It was not easy for us to lift our big, muscular, eighty-two-pound dog.

While one leg was worse, both front legs were affected. Dr. Rao took X-rays and we looked at them on the monitor. There appeared to be no bone damage other than the elbow dysplasia, which existed long before this. So what was causing Lakota's pain was some kind of soft-tissue injury. The problem was my dog couldn't walk and we couldn't hold him up for long periods of time. How would he relieve himself? We struggled for a week with aching backs, hoping the injury would heal. But there was no improvement in his condition.

Fortunately, our vet still had some tricks up her sleeve. She suggested we try PRP, also known as Platelet-rich Plasma. This was a new, non-surgical treatment that had been used with some success on athletes to help heal injuries and get them back to functioning form. It involved drawing blood from the patient, separating the platelets from other blood cells, and concentrating them. Then the concentrated platelet plasma was combined with the remaining blood and injected into the sites of injury. There were no guarantees and little research had been done on its effectiveness. However, it was nonsurgical and required just sedation and, since it was Lakota's own blood, there was no risk of a reaction. Some very famous athletes had been successfully treated with it and we were up against a wall with Lakota, who was not getting better. Anything that could help him heal faster was worth a try.

Like the stem cell treatment, after this Lakota would have to be on a leash for an extended period of time, and we would have be very careful to not allow any impact on his front legs till he was healed. He would also need physical therapy, but my vet would teach me how to do it and I could do it for Lakota at home. Because we still had all the aids we had made from a few years back when our boy had his stem cell surgery, we could easily set up the house to keep him from hurting himself. We scheduled the treatment for the next morning.

The procedure went smoothly and we brought Lakota home that afternoon. Because he had not been under anesthesia for as long duration as for the stem cell procedure, he recovered from the sedation fairly quickly and even ate his dinner—broken up into several smaller meals. We helped him out to relieve himself after dinner and before bed. He still didn't want to use his front legs. He kept one up in the air and hopped painfully on the other, while we held most of the weight off of the leg with the lifting harness to avoid injuring it.

The next morning, things were pretty much the same. But in the afternoon, we got a wonderful surprise when we took our wounded warrior out to relieve himself. He wanted to lie down on the grass in the sun, so we let him. We sat by him on the patio and, after a few minutes, he got up on his own and walked away from us to the other side of the yard, using both of his front legs quite normally. As with the stem cell treatment, Lakota had healed rapidly and beyond expectations. I put his leash on to make sure, if he saw a chipmunk, he didn't run after it. We had weeks of slow leash walks and physical therapy ahead, but compared to having to lift and hold up an eighty-two pound dog, I was actually looking forward to it.

After the first few days, I decided that my boy had cabin fever and needed to get out more. We put him in the back of the SUV using a ramp and drove him to the park for the first time since his PRP. Elaine and Cooper were to meet us there and we would take a very short leash walk and then take Lakota home. It was a beautiful day, and we could just hang out there and let Lakota lie in the sun for a little while, too.

When we arrived, Elaine and Cooper were already there. Cooper was at the beginning of the trail, unleashed, standing with his "dog mom." I went around to the back of the SUV and opened the door, preparing to get the ramp out of the rear seat and put it in place. But Cooper had other ideas. Before anyone could stop him, he leaped into the back of the SUV because he couldn't wait one more minute to see his buddy. He settled down next to Lakota and snuggled his head on Lakota's back. It was obvious how happy the two dogs were to see one another. We let them just enjoy being together for a while and then put the ramp in to get them both out. We were anxious for Lakota to do his business since the lack of exercise was making that a concern. We walked a very short distance, and, sure enough, the smells on the trail got things moving and we accomplished our mission.

By then, Lakota had walked enough. I got one of the floor mats out of the SUV and laid it on the blacktop so the tired dog had a comfortable place to lie down, and he did so. A minute later, Cooper came over and, once again, lay down right next to his buddy. Cooper could have been walking the trail, smelling the good smells and greeting other dogs and people and doing all sorts of exciting things, but he made it clear he would rather lie next to his buddy. It was so touching to see the affection these two grown male dogs had for each other.

Lakota was a cooperative patient. He allowed me to ice the areas that needed it and manipulate his legs for his P.T. as my vet had taught me to do. We checked off everything on our "to do" list and as the weeks passed, Lakota gradually got better. We were blessed that Lakota's athletic, muscular body had responded so well to both the stem cell and the PRP, because not all dogs do. Lakota had dodged another bullet. As I mentioned before, arthritis is one of the most frequent reasons for dogs having to be euthanized. Cats may have nine lives, but it was looking very much like my Labrador was on his third.

Before anyone could stop him, Cooper leaped into the back of the SUV because he couldn't wait one more minute to see his buddy.

The exhausted dog would not go inside without doing his job one last time, and he headed for the mailbox to get the newspaper.

CHAPTER SEVENTEEN:

Losing Battle: March 2016

In January, we celebrated Lakota's twelfth birthday. But all was not well. It started with him waking up at night, panting loudly. It was cool in our room. Something was wrong, and I knew panting could mean pain. I took him to the vet the next day. X-rays of his lungs revealed them to be freckled with black dots. We sent the X-rays to be evaluated by an oncologist. He said it was nothing to worry about—just old-dog lungs. We accidently discovered that lying on a cold gel mat, which we had bought for Zeak when he had a fever, stopped the panting attacks. So we put one on the bed and one in the living room for him. But it was a mystery why it helped.

In a previous chapter, I noted that Lakota had been doing something for some time, every single night, that had me wondering what was going on. Around seven or seven-thirty he would get up from his cooling mat, sit across from me, and stare at me intently. He used to do this around ten p.m., when it was time for last out, and then we went to bed. But now he wanted me to go to bed three hours earlier. I couldn't do that. I was an insomniac and that would mess up my sleep schedule, which was sure to trigger a long bout of sleeplessness. But he was relentless. I asked him to stop but he wouldn't. He kept staring at me till I could feel his eyes burning holes in me and I couldn't stand it anymore. I didn't want to give in, because it was now difficult and painful for him to get into bed and I didn't want him to go through it twice. And it wasn't healthy for him to hold everything in from seven p.m. till six a.m. I finally decided to do what he wanted me to, and to keep his lifting harness on so we could help him back out of bed for last out, and then back in. He seemed content with this arrangement, and if it was worth it for him to do an extra climb in and out of bed, he must have really wanted this for some reason. I watched TV or read in bed.

Then Lakota started having serious digestion problems. We treated it palliatively, to avoid anything invasive or painful. Then one day he stopped eating. Lakota had never refused food in his life. Again, we took him right to the vet. She gave him medication. Next he started gagging loudly, occasionally, for no apparent reason. When he finally resumed eating, he vomited. When he didn't respond quickly to treatment, we were referred to a specialist. In order to find out what the problem was, Lakota would have to be put under anesthesia and scoped. I didn't want to put him through anesthesia at his age, but it wouldn't be painful, and we had no choice: He was losing a pound a day of muscle. Our athletic, muscular dog was wasting away before our eyes.

The diagnosis was inflammatory bowel disease and lymphangiectasia. I had never heard of the latter. Lymphangiectasia is a horrible disease where dogs starve to death because they can't digest or absorb food. In Lakota's case it was secondary to the inflammatory bowel disease and in early stages, so since the IBD was treatable, we should still have some time left before the unthinkable would happen.

Our specialist got the digestive issues under control quickly, despite Lakota's sensitivities to various medicines. We had a third vet—a veterinary nutritionist—formulate a home-cooked diet, because we wanted our dog to have the best food possible…real food and nothing processed. We were making massive amounts of food, because Lakota was ravenous now that his stomach felt better, and he needed to gain weight. He was consuming ten cups of food a day, and we were working nearly full time to make it.

Bill was roasting turkey breasts with the skin removed, and roasting eye rounds of beef, cutting the fat out of them, and grinding them. Lakota had to eat a very low-fat diet. I was cooking, peeling, and mashing massive amounts of sweet potatoes, and getting strange looks at Costco and the supermarket, checking out with nothing but enormous quantities of sweet potatoes. I bought a rice cooker to cook the huge quantities of rice needed. I was also spending half a day each week fixing his medications: I cut all his pills in half with a pill splitter and stuffed them into empty capsules I got at a compounding pharmacy. That way I could hide them in his food so he wouldn't taste them, and I wouldn't have to shove pills down his throat. No living thing would want that done to them.

While it was a tough regimen, we were thrilled, because Lakota was so much better…or so it seemed. We set clear limits with the specialist: We wanted to keep

Lakota with us as long as possible, *if* he could have a good quality of life. However, we made guidelines clear to the vets: no invasive or painful treatments, because we would not allow Lakota to suffer or be frightened. We went on for a couple of months like this and Lakota seemed to be having a good quality of life.

Then the other shoe dropped. A routine blood test turned up a shockingly low red blood cell count. His bone marrow had stopped making red blood cells. The specialist, a veterinary internist, tried two immune-suppressing drugs to help. Both made Lakota sick. Then he tried a hormone that should have stimulated Lakota's bone marrow to start working, but it didn't. As the non-regenerative anemia worsened, we reached the point where soon, Lakota would be incredibly weak and short of breath. A lot of people aren't aware of this, but shortness of breath is ranked higher than the highest level of pain on the animal hospice scale. It creates such an incredible anxiety/panic it is even used for torture of humans. That was the wall our back was up against. The internist offered us two options.

The first was a bone biopsy to diagnose the problem. It would be done under general anesthesia, but still would produce pain—sometimes intense pain—afterward. Lakota had a condition called "wind-up"—a pain syndrome that made it likely that he would have terrible pain from this procedure. I refused to let them do it. This meant they had to treat without diagnosing the cause. But I already suspected the cause of all of these illnesses. I could feel the dragon-snake making its presence known. Lakota was getting too sick from the medications, anyway. We, who are our pet's guardians, need to think through how much medical treatment is humane to subject our animals to. Would they choose these painful, sometimes terrifying procedures? I was not going to put him through hell because I couldn't let go of him. That is not what love looks like to me.

The second option was transfusions. This meant twenty-four hours or more each time, hospitalized in a cage. Transfusions are very tricky and dangerous for dogs. He would feel sick and frightened and it could be life-threatening. He could die alone in a cage in the hospital without his family to comfort him. And it would only last a week or two and have to keep being repeated. There was no way I was going to do this to my dog.

Lakota was at the top end of the average life of a Labrador Retriever, which was ten to twelve years. I wanted him to be with me another hundred years! But that was not going to happen, and something awful was coming at us very fast. None of the alternatives were acceptable, or even promising. I had to protect him from suffering. I believe we owe our animals that. So I did the thing I most didn't want to do: The thing I would have done anything that didn't hurt my dog, to prevent. I made an appointment with a veterinary home euthanasia specialist. I wanted Lakota to have the most loving, peaceful, gentle passing I could give him...even though what I really wanted with all my heart, was to not have to let him go.

But I could not be selfish and keep him here and watch him struggle to get air. I made the first available appointment, which was for the following week, praying for help and guidance to time it so it would happen just as the symptoms of the low red blood cells hit. If it got bad before then, I would have to take him to the emergency vet; so I had everything staged and ready to do that at a moment's notice. I didn't want to lose one good day with him by doing it too early, but I knew that doing it one day too late would be far worse and cause unbearable suffering.

I did not leave him for even a moment that week. I had bought a slew of dog toys the week before, and I gave him a new one every day. Lakota loved getting a new toy. He would explore it with his mouth, hoping to find squeakers and grunters. I fed him smaller meals more often, to avoid tummy upsets and also because he loved to eat. When he felt up to it, we went out in the yard or took short walks on the trail. I lay on the floor with him, snuggled up against his warm body. I gave him gentle massages. I was grateful for every moment I could be with him. I remembered how awful it was when I had to let go of Santana—my Labrador from many years ago—while I was working and couldn't get time off to spend with him. I still bear the guilt from that. Our animals are our family for many of us. We need bereavement time when we lose them. It is brutal, and I was not the only teacher in our school who had to return to work and lost it in front of a class because they did not have time to heal after the loss of a pet. I have a friend who is a health care worker, who was in the same situation not long ago.

Two days before the appointed day, early in the morning, I took Lakota to the beginning of the upper trail to the dam, which was right behind our house. My intention was to just go a few feet down the trail, and then come back. I asked Bill to come along in case Lakota needed help coming back. Nothing will ever convince me that Lakota didn't know this would be his last walk. He totally rejected the short walk idea, despite his debilitated condition. He kept wanting to go a little further and a little further, and so on...until I realized that my dog was determined to go to the dam, one last time. I decided to let him do as he wished. I told Bill I would ask him to go get the car and meet us at the end of the short trail if Lakota couldn't make it back. I don't know how my dog found the strength, but he made it to the dam. He savored every smell and sight along the way, taking his time—and I did likewise. We stood on the dam overlooking the water, and I cried buckets. Then we started the trip back.

The trip home was slow. Every step was hard work for my boy, and we took numerous rests. When we reached our yard, I lay on the grass with him to rest a while. It was early spring, and the grass was already green and soft. After we rested we got up, and it was my intention to take my dog right into the house, the back way, which had fewer steps. But again, Lakota had other ideas. This exhausted dog would not go inside without doing his job one last time, and he headed for the mailbox to get the newspaper. He reached up into the newspaper tube and took the paper out. Five times on the way in, he stopped to lie down and rest. Each time I tried to take the paper from him to relieve him of carrying it, but he was adamant. He brought it all the way into the house and dropped it at my feet. Then he collapsed into a deep sleep.

Later that afternoon, I had invited some of Lakota's friends to come to say goodbye. Most of them had seen him by three o'clock, when Elaine and Cooper came up. My friend Cathy from up the street, who had stayed

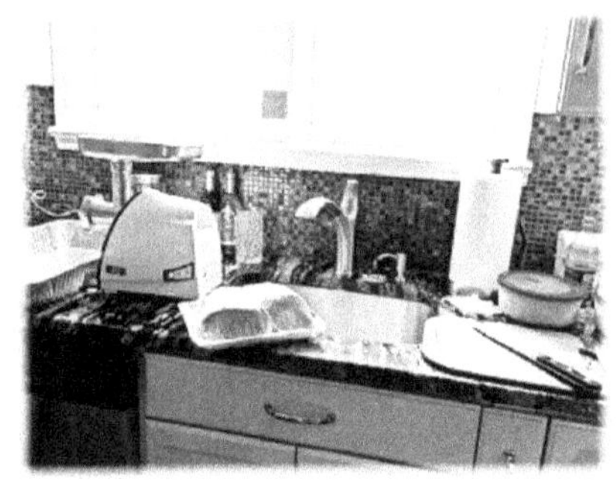

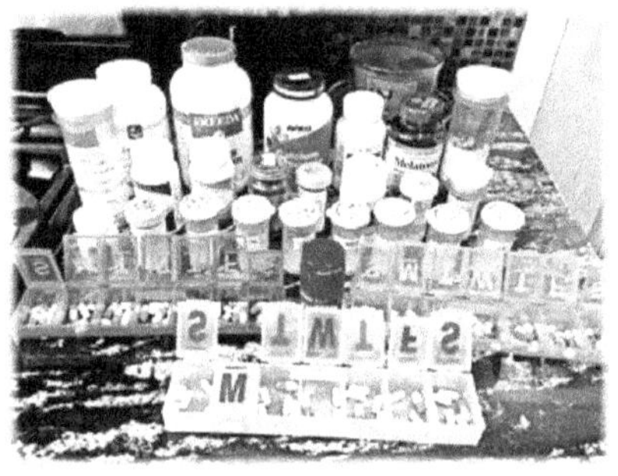

We were cooking a special low fat diet for Lakota, and cutting all his pills up and stuffing them into capsules from a compounding pharmacy, so we could hide them in his food.

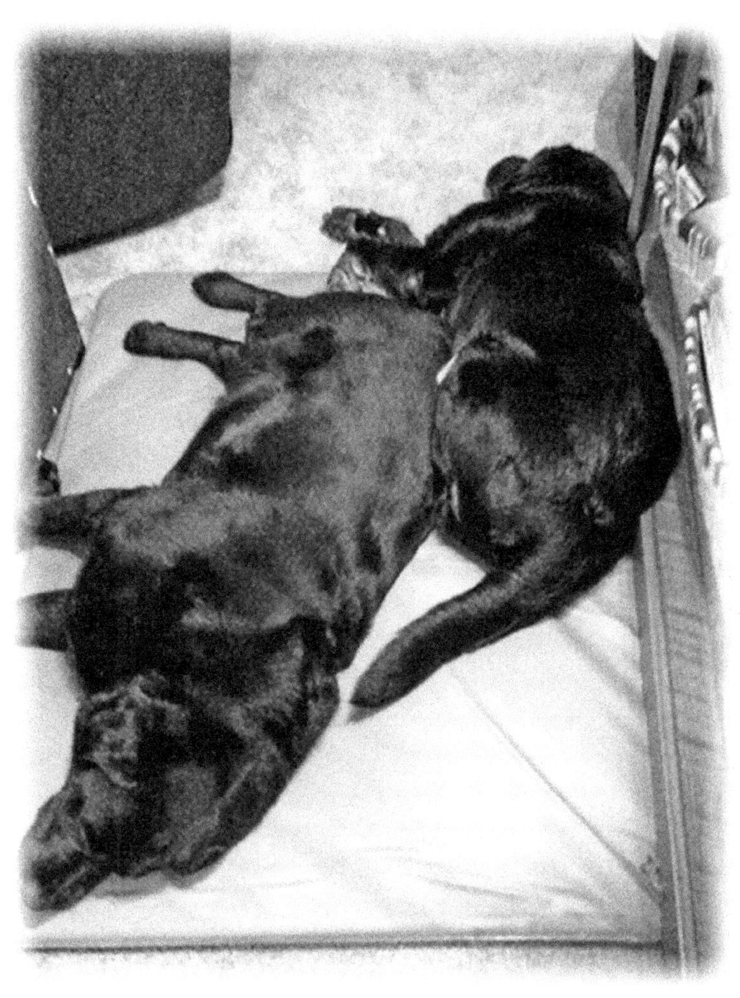

I don't know what Cooper did with his legs,
and it couldn't have been comfortable,
but there he stayed.

with my dogs when I was going to be out a long time, also came to say goodbye. A few minutes later, our dog walker—who had walked Lakota and Zeak anytime I was sick or injured, came by with her recently born baby girl.

The dog walker knew dogs well and knew Lakota well. What she did next spoke magnitudes about Lakota's character. She sat on the floor and put her newborn in her carrier down on the floor, right next to Lakota. Then she allowed Lakota to say hello to her little girl, which he did, in full therapy-dog mode. Ever so gently and ever so carefully, he tenderly sniffed the baby and gave her a gentle kiss on top of her head. Then he lay down next to her. "There are very few dogs I would trust this much." she said.

I was so glad to have this particular group of people here. It was such a comfort, because they kept a casual, upbeat conversation going while we petted the dogs, drank iced tea, and acted as though it was just a normal day. It helped me to pass the time without thinking too much and gave me a break from the mounting dread I had been feeling.

After a while, Lakota moved to the cooling mat. He lay down on it and stretched out to sleep. His buddy Cooper went over to join him. Lakota had pretty much passed out and that did not leave room for Cooper, but Cooper squeezed in anyway, wanting to be close to his brother-in-heart. I don't know what he did with his legs, and it couldn't have been comfortable, but there he stayed.

The visit came to an end, and I set about making dinner. As night approached, I wondered how I could possibly spend tomorrow—the last full day I would have Lakota with me—so it would be enough. Of course I knew the answer to that question was there was no way that I could ever have enough time with him. But I had set aside that day to spend with my boy alone.

We spent that day in a state of meditation—just being...being together as I soaked up the feeling of his "essence" so I would be able to recognize him if he came to me in his spirit body...recognize him after I crossed over myself someday. It was an entire day that lasted only a moment—a moment spent just cherishing one another, in a wordless state of unquestioning, unconditional love.

I know my dog is dying.
So what could he possibly be seeing
that is making him smile?

CHAPTER EIGHTEEN:

The Escort: March 28, 2016

It is what it is. And this is as bad as it gets. Today I have to let Lakota go. I have known this day was coming for five days. But nothing could prepare me for it. I sit on the floor of my bedroom next to Lakota, already somewhat in shock because of what is coming. Suddenly Lakota sits up and starts to follow something around the room with his eyes. He is smiling and following some moving thing with his eyes that is totally invisible to me. For no reason, my gaze is diverted to my night table. What catches my eye is the picture of Lakota and Zeak in a frame that sits on the table. Only something has happened to it: It has somehow slid out of the frame and is tipped over on its side. It has been in that frame for ten years. And it slides out today for no reason—on this most awful of days when I am going to do the unthinkable?

I know my dog is dying. I know he is in pain. I know he is so weak he can barely move. So what could he possibly be seeing that is making him smile? And, jumping up like he did had to hurt, and take energy he didn't have. As I pose this question in my mind, I am reminded of something I was told by a hospice nurse once, many years ago. She told me it had been her experience that as people drew very close to dying, many of them had "visits" from the spirits of loved ones who had left the physical world before them. When this happened, she would always tell their families sitting with them that the time was probably near. As the thought of what this nurse had told me crossed my mind, as an explanation of what was going on in the room, it brought back a memory.

A few years ago, my godmother and favorite aunt was nearing the end of her life. She was ninety-six years old and not enjoying her life any more. While she was very clear and sharp mentally, physically, all she could do was lie on the couch or in bed, and watch TV. She was in pain all the time and was struggling to get enough air. She and I had an authentic, honest relationship, and so she had no problem telling me that she had enough of this world and was ready to go on.

Every Friday afternoon I would go visit her and bring coffee and a donut for her. (OK, I brought one for me too!) On the Friday afternoon I was remembering, she was quite agitated when I arrived. I took off my coat, handed her goodies to her, sat down, and asked her what was wrong.

"It's the people upstairs!" she said, noticeably upset.

I found this quite confusing, since my aunt lived in a ranch house. So I asked her, gently, what people she was referring to, since there was no upstairs.

In an impatient and annoyed tone, she said, "You know…THE PEOPLE UPSTAIRS! My sisters and the rest of them…they are very excited that I am coming to be with them. But they are making such an awful racket it's terrible. I can't even rest!"

Her four sisters had died years ago, so now I knew who the people upstairs were. And judging from what the nurse had told me years before, my aunt was soon to cross over. And so it was. At eleven p.m., her caretaker looked in on her and found her sitting up in bed, smiling and chuckling to herself. When the caretaker asked her why she was so happy, my aunt told her that God had come to tell her she could finally go to be with Him, and she was so happy about that… and fearless. She died around three a.m. with a smile on her face.

And so, on this most terrible of mornings, with the most terrible of tasks ahead of me, my dog, Lakota, was following something around the room with a joyful smile on his beautiful face. When I noticed the picture out of the frame, I knew what he was smiling about: His beloved, adopted brother, The Zeakie Dog, had come to take Lakota home.

He was slipping in and out of
an unusually deep sleep.

CHAPTER NINETEEN:

Saying Goodbye: March 28, 2016

On the day that was to be the final day, Dr. Rao came by our home before work to say goodbye to Lakota. She stayed with him, massaging him, for a long time—I knew he was special to her. That was one of the two reasons guiding my decision to not have her be the person to put him down. The other reason was that I had heard of problems with euthanasia. It wasn't common, but it wasn't rare either. I wanted to be sure it went painlessly and I wanted to be sure—absolutely sure—that my dog had passed. I therefore had made arrangements for a veterinary euthanasia specialist to come to our home, so Lakota would be where he was comfortable as we helped him to cross over. Afterwards, I had arranged to bring his body to Dr. Rao whom I trusted implicitly. I wanted him to be examined, so I had two vets agree that he was deceased and not in some comatose state. I had heard that Animals First—the facility where our specialists were—always had two vets examine their patients after euthanasia to be sure the process was complete. I would do no less for Lakota.

It was time for Dr. Rao to leave for work. She had spent a lot of time with Lakota, and told me that he was not himself anymore and that I was making the right decision. I didn't know it then, but she was saving my sanity, because Lakota wasn't going to make it easy, and I was desperately going to need to have heard that it was the right time to let him go. She is one special person.

It was apparent that my dog was in bad shape. He was now tranfusional, meaning his red cell count had dropped so low he should be given a transfusion. He would start having those awful suffocation symptoms if we didn't give him blood very soon. He was slipping in and out of an unusually deep sleep—so deep that I actually had the feeling that he might pass naturally before the euthanasia vet came at noon. As long as it wasn't painful, that would have been so much easier on me than to have to make that agonizing decision. I had to remind myself that not getting enough air is above the highest degree of pain on the hospice pain scale. It was imperative that I not forget this.

Our vet said her loving goodbye and left. At noon, right on time, the euthanasia vet and her tech arrived. They set up in the bedroom while I stayed with Lakota. I wanted Lakota to be in the place he would feel most comfortable when he "left"—on our bed where he slept every night. I had specially prepared the bed ahead of time for this with waterproof bedding covered by soft, cuddly bedding. Every last detail of how I did this was about what was best for him—period. He deserved no less than that.

An hour and a half later I was still struggling to give the command for Lakota to follow me into the bedroom. We had given him a last meal of all his favorite foods that he hadn't been allowed for a long time. The vet had been very patient and kind, but I couldn't delay her any longer. I had decided I would stay calm no matter what, so Lakota would not be additionally frightened by my emotions. Feeling like I was going to get sick, I calmly called him to come with me into the bedroom. He sat up, smiled, and gave me an "I'm fine—we can't do this because I'm-not-leaving-you-look." I have no doubt at all that he knew exactly what was going to happen in that room. I called him a second time. Same thing—he held his ground. It was unbearable—he didn't want to go. I called him a third time and said, "C'mon, baby—we have to do this. There is terrible suffering ahead and I can't let that happen to you. I love you too much."

Lakota obeyed. He got on the bed. I held him in my arms and looked into his eyes and gave the vet the go-ahead. I told my beautiful companion how much I loved him, and I thanked him for all his love, loyalty, protection, hard work, and help. I stayed calm for him as my heart broke. I loved him with all my might, as we helped him leave his sick body.

He went peacefully as I held him in my arms. There was no profound spiritual experience as there had been with Zeak. There was nothing. That upset me, because Zeak left me with such a mind-blowing occurrence that there was no room for doubt. I knew he was going on. I knew he was still around. But Lakota's quiet, uneventful passing left me with questions. Was Zeak some special, advanced soul that he could do what he did? Did that mean that Lakota wouldn't know how to or be able to contact me? That thought made me fall into a deep pit of sorrow.

Lakota's quiet, uneventful passing
left me with questions.

When Zeak was put down, I was practically begging the vet to do it because of the serious suffering that was occurring. Here, I was doing it *before* the awful suffering. It was much kinder for my dog, but hell for me. I was now very glad that my vet had come and supported this decision, or I might be second-guessing myself. Looking back, I know that while this was both the most gut-wrenching and the most unselfish thing I have ever done, that did not ease my heartbreak at the time. But even with all that pain, what was going to happen in a little while would reassure me that what I had done was *the right thing at exactly the right time, beyond a shadow of a doubt*. Because something else was going on in Lakota's body—something none of the tests had detected.

As the vet and her tech put Lakota on a stretcher to carry him to their SUV, an unexpected thing occurred. A fluid tinged with blood began pouring out of Lakota's nose—a lot of fluid. The vet told us—in a surprised tone—that this was *NOT* normal. Days later, I spoke to my vet and the specialist. They could only guess, but the best guess was cancer—in the lungs or sinuses or maybe in internal lymph nodes, undetectable—that had rapidly spread through Lakota's body and into his bone marrow, causing the anemia. At that moment I remembered something from when Zeak had lymphoma: I remembered that at the end, cancer cells can fill the lungs with fluid in minutes, causing a horrible death by suffocation. If that was what was happening here, it is possible that we averted that *right before it happened*.

After the specialist left, we brought Lakota's body to Dr. Rao. She climbed into the back of the SUV with a stethoscope, examined Lakota, and confirmed that he had passed. We had made arrangements at an animal crematorium ahead of time. We called them and advised them that we were heading up there with Lakota's body. When we arrived, we were treated with kindness and compassion. It was a beautiful place, but nothing was going to console us now.

For the next week I was hit with the full brunt of grieving for my beloved family member, partner, and best friend. The loving presence that was at my side every minute was gone. It was devastating. I was too sick to my stomach leave the house for a week. I was putting one foot in front of the other, trying so hard to go on, despite feeling lost, sad, and broken without my companion. One thing I knew for sure: This was *not* the time to get another dog. It would not be fair to inflict this painful energy on a new dog. Dogs are not replaceable or interchangeable, any more than beloved human family members are.

But then, little things started to happen—synchronicities—that reassured me that Lakota was OK and even around. And soon after, I was to be blessed with some extraordinary contacts. As he had helped me when he was here, he was about to help me from the other side. It reminded me that, although I have no idea how long I will walk this Earth, I know full well that, as long as I do, *I am walking with two shadows.*

P.S. to the subject of this chapter

If you go back to page 150 in this chapter, you will notice I said I "struggled" with giving the go-ahead for an hour and a half. Because I was having such a difficult time recovering, I went to a grief therapy session. I learned something very important that I want to pass on. Well, it turns out that getting "stuck" in a highly stressful situation like that is a trigger for trauma. I was having to overcome trauma as well as grief. Whether you decide to do a home euthanasia or one at a vet's office, spend time with your animal before, but once the vet arrives or you arrive at the vet's, do not delay—proceed immediately. People underestimate the severity of a situation like this—it can even cause PTSD. Avoid putting yourself in a situation where you have an unspecified amount of time before you "give the order." Prearrange it that way with your vet. The vet is in a difficult position and can't appear to be rushing you at a time like that, so be proactive and both protect yourself *and* do the kind thing for your animal.

I offer a final caution: Make sure you thoroughly investigate whom you choose to euthanize your dog, and where your pet's body will be processed. It is not unheard of for animals to be sedated and then wind up in the wrong hands—terribly wrong hands. I would like to think this is uncommon, but it should be unthinkable that it could happen at all.

One of my dogs was sending me a signal that Lakota was OK.

CHAPTER TWENTY:

Signals: April 6, 2016

It is the day after Lakota's passing. I am too devastated—both emotionally and physically—to do anything but alternately cry and distract myself by watching mindless TV. At four o'clock, I am getting nauseous from not eating, so I tell Bill that I need to eat something. I suggest we go to an off-the-beaten-path diner because I am a mess and don't want to see anyone I know. I do not want to make conversation. I just want to eat comfort food and I don't have the energy to make it.

We get into the SUV, and I immediately notice that my navigator holder has fallen off the windshield and knocked down the little stuffed, black Labrador Retriever that is my car mascot. That has never happened before. The navigator holder has fallen off, but it has never fallen near or on the stuffed dog and it was there all the time. The mascot has been there with me for twelve years, since I got Lakota, both in this vehicle and the SUV that was totaled in the accident.

We drive to the diner. I wear sunglasses to hide my red, swollen eyes. We sit down in a booth and have not said a word when the server, a young man, greets us with, "What a beautiful day! I took my dog in the woods this morning."

There are people who would never notice the synchronicity of those two events: two things that have never happened in my life, both happening in succession, and both about dogs. One a stuffed version of my dog and one, a dog being taken in the woods in the morning—something Lakota and I did every single morning—I took notice. I have never had a server greet me like that. Ever. One of my dogs was sending me a signal that Lakota was OK.

I am not an experienced medium. I am an empath: I am learning how to do this, and I am having some real success. So far, however, I have no control over when I get contacts from my animals. It is always a surprise when it happens. I think there is something about trying too hard for this communion that sabotages success. It always happens when I am in a relaxed, peaceful state. Sometimes I am distracted, doing something non-stressful, like hanging ornaments on my Christmas tree, hiking, or driving on a country road. I have had contacts happen at those times. One thing I am convinced of is that spirits will not come to us when we are angry, frustrated, lashing out, or projecting any kind of negative energy.

No doubt existed in my mind
that this was absolutely
the best birthday gift I had ever received.

CHAPTER TWENTY-ONE:

Happy Birthday to Me: April 12, 2016

It's my birthday today, but certainly not a happy one. I am still devastated by the loss of Lakota. The prospect of living my life without my boy is heart-wrenching, but I can't even think about another dog. My girlfriends are trying to cheer me up, and the distraction is helpful, but it always comes back to me being here and him being there, and I miss him more than any words could possibly say.

At night I am too exhausted to do anything, so I collapse in my recliner in front of the TV like a boneless blob, and alternately watch whatever can drown out the pain, and doze. I had fallen asleep for an indeterminate amount of time when something woke me up. I looked around to see what had intruded on my sleep. It hadn't startled me—I was just aware that something had clearly aroused me—when I saw him. It was strikingly clear: an almost solid, with just the slightest hint of transparency, visual image of Lakota very close to me—just a little lower than my face. He was on the arm of the recliner and his face was about a foot from my face. It was clear and detailed. He was perfect and beautiful and young—in his prime, in fact. No grey hair. Not a trace of sickness. He was flawless and happy and peaceful and well, and as I realized that this was a real "visit," I was filled with peace and gratitude. The image lasted about five or six seconds and it moved slightly in a natural way—the way a dog would if it were lying down and just hanging around. Tears of joy spilled onto my face, and ran down my cheeks and all over my shirt. No doubt existed in my mind that this was absolutely the best birthday gift I had ever received.

Before this, I didn't think anything could console me or make me feel better. I alternated between devastating bouts of grief that had actually made me physically ill, and working on anything and everything that I had the energy to do, in order to distract myself from the pain. I had also been experiencing intense bouts of a gnawing pain in my stomach, accompanied by periods of nausea and an inability to eat. But Lakota coming through to me like this and seeing him so perfect, and well, and peaceful, and beautiful, was genuinely helpful. I thanked him from the bottom of my being. I have heard it takes a lot of energy to pull off something like this, and he had barely had time to fully transition. But it was so totally like Lakota to want to "Help Mommy!" Any time I had used those words with him it would generate joy and excitement in him. That was always his favorite thing to do. And this time he has helped me more than words can say.

My animals seem to make an attempt to visit me or send me signs or symbols on special occasions. Christmas, my birthday, their birthdays, Mother's Day, and their crossover days (the days they passed) are often acknowledged in some way near that day. This year, three days after Zeak's crossover day, I awoke to the electric candle on the mantel being on. It hasn't been on since last Christmas season. I didn't turn it on. It wasn't on when I went to bed. My husband said it wasn't on when he went to bed. There is no way we could have missed it in the dark room. But there was no missing it when I got up, since it was right opposite my face in the pre-sunrise, dark living room.

These contacts don't seem to happen exactly on the day of the occasion, but rather near it. I have been told by several mediums—people I was confident truly had that gift—that time is different where our deceased pets are, so it is difficult for them to pinpoint dates here. Some have even said there is no time there. I can't really grasp what that means.

In this photograph, shot through the screen door,
Lakota goes out and lies on the back porch,
watching the world go by, like he used to.

CHAPTER TWENTY-TWO:

All I Have to Do Is Dream: April 17, 2016

It will be three weeks this coming Monday since Lakota crossed over. I am having serious stomach issues. The very sensitivities that make me able to perceive my animals' spirits also make me very vulnerable to suffering. It's not easy being like this. I am not sure I would have made it this long without serious medical consequences without the amazing help I have gotten from Lakota. Last night I had another remarkable visit.

I am asleep this time, and he comes to me in a dream. He is lying on my bed and I throw his red ball to him. He catches it and is all happy, energetic, and ready to play. As he was the last time he came through to me, he is this time: young, beautiful, and healthy. Dream visits are much more vivid than ordinary dreams. Like a modern TV, they are in high definition. The red ball is so red it almost hurts! In my dream I am so happy that he is well and up for playing. My friend Peggy, who passed away a year ago, is also visiting, and is there on the other side of the bed. I am now aware I am dreaming—a lucid dream—and we start moving through the house. In my dream it is dark in the house, as it is in reality—it's the middle of the night. However, the darkness has a distinctively blue cast, and we can see clearly with no lights on, as Lakota leads me out of my bedroom. We move through the house, floating parallel to, but without touching the ground, and go to the back door. Lakota goes out and lies on the back porch, watching the world go by, like he used to. I stay in and watch him…like I used to.

At this point, I wake up. I am so happy that I have received another visit. I decide that as long as I am awake, I might as well get up and use the bathroom. I am just about to do that when I feel it: the firm pressure of a large dog pressing up against me, lying beside me in bed. I feel the warmth emanating from his body. I feel the solid mass of his body—something I have also heard is very difficult for spirits to manifest. This is the icing on the cake of this visit! I am filled with gratitude and so in awe that Lakota could do this. I think he knows I am deeply devastated and is helping me all he can. And he IS helping.

I always was afraid that Lakota was a younger soul than Zeak and that when he passed he wouldn't know how to stay in touch. I had read that it was easier for older souls to do these things. The thought of being out of contact was unbearable. I had underestimated my dog. He, like The Zeakie Dog, is a master at this, and has pulled off two stunning visits in a week!

At what point does a coincidence become a synchronicity? This is a message from Lakota!

CHAPTER TWENTY-THREE:

This Is Not Just a Walk in the Park: June 13, 2016

I am day-caring Cooper this week while Elaine is visiting family out of state. I am still grieving the loss of my beloved Lakota, and taking our morning hike in the woods on a beautiful spring day makes me miss him even more. I suspect his buddy, Cooper, is missing him almost as much as I am. I feel particularly close to Cooper now, because we are both feeling the loss of Lakota. In their prime, these two black Labradors would have been tearing through the woods together, jumping over fallen trees in a joyous game of tag. But with Lakota gone and Cooper entering his senior years, those days were over. Cooper quietly and unenthusiastically follows behind me off-leash, on the trail, both his head and his tail low.

As we are walking down the trail, a tall stranger—male—is coming up the trail. I ask him if he is comfortable with dogs or if he would like me to leash Cooper—I tell him Cooper is a polite, friendly dog and will not jump on him. He declines to have me leash Cooper, and continues on his way without further conversation. We finish our hike and head home to give Cooper his lunch and have ours as well.

The next day, we set out on our daily hike again, with a reluctant Cooper in tow. Cooper misses both his mommy and his buddy, and would prefer to wait on the couch, but *that option is not good for him or for me, so I insist that he come with us. Once he gets rolling and his nose takes over, I know he will enjoy the walk. As we climb the first steep hill on the trail, the same stranger we met the day before passes us from behind, but today, without a word, he hands me a piece of paper as he walks by. This is quite surprising, since I don't know him and don't remember ever seeing him before yesterday. What is on the paper is even more surprising. It is a poem about a dog, written by American poet Mark Doty. At the end of the poem, it calls the dog a "Zen-*master.*" I instantly recognize this as what it is: a message from Lakota!*

The reason I feel this is a message from Lakota is that the use of the word "master" to describe a dog is highly unusual, and I had recently received another communication with that word describing my dog. When Lakota passed, Dr. Rao sent me a sympathy card on which she wrote a Haiku about Lakota. She wrote:

"Gentle, kind, healing,
The spirit of Lakota
Rests within us now.

With respect, love, and humility, I join you in mourning the loss of your beloved Lakota. He truly was a Master.*"*

At the end of the poem, she called him a "master." "What are the odds? I ask myself. "How often have I heard or read of a dog described as a 'master?" Exactly no times, I answer myself. At what point does a coincidence become a synchronicity? This is a message from Lakota! I am feeling the exhilaration that always comes from a spiritual contact. I am revved as I walk down the rest of the trail.

As I approached my car in the parking lot, I saw the man again. I walked over and thanked him, saying, "You may not know this, but that was not only a poem…it was a message from my dog, who has passed, but still connects with me."

What the man had to say next left me even more convinced that this was Lakota's work.

"And I was the messenger!" he responded. He then told me that after seeing me on the trail the day before, for some unexplainable reason, he thought of me that evening and was "strongly moved" to look up that particular poem—which was by one of his favorite poets—and to print it out and come to the park to give it to me the next day. A total stranger is "strongly moved" upon seeing someone to turn on his computer, find a particular poem, and go through the trouble of printing it out, seeking me out, and giving it to me. I found that extraordinary, especially since we never spoke a word! He then added something else, "They're saving us, you know."

I asked if he meant animals in general, and he answered in the affirmative. I had heard and read that there are people who believe animals are bearing a lot of the karma of human beings, to save us from destroying our own planet. Apparently, this stranger was one of them. I was inclined to agree with this line of thought—I had just always put it in the context of our individual animals taking on our burdens of illness, stress, and emotions. I have had several vets tell me that they are surprised how many of their animal clients are on the same medications for the same reasons that their owners are. Renowned holistic veterinarian Dr. Martin Goldstein, D.V.M., discusses some of these occurrences in his book The Nature of Animal Healing. *He has had spiritual experiences of his own with animals, which he also describes in his book.*

I believe our animals take these illnesses on to serve and help their owners by sharing some of their burdens. But I believe the man in the parking lot meant what he said in a global context, as well.

As our conversation concluded, I thanked him, telling him that the message made my day and brought me joy and comfort in my grief. He said it was his pleasure. It was many months before I saw him again at the park, which made the odds of our having run in to each other, and of him delivering a lovely message from Lakota, even more surprising. He wasn't here at the same time that I was I was very often.

One of the messages I have gotten from Lakota several times is that of a heart.

CHAPTER TWENTY-FOUR:

Validation: June 28, 2016

I have been reading everything I can on animal communication and meditating. Once a week I do meditations for each of my dogs, and I keep journals and record the images they send me. One of the images I have gotten from Lakota several times is that of a heart. I send thoughts to Lakota several times a day. I am anxious to determine if my communication attempts are reaching him, so I ask him to send me a physical manifestation of a heart when he is able to, in order to confirm that he is getting my messages. I ask for a heart because he has sent me that symbol before, so I associate that image with him.

Two days later, as I am awakening, I see an exquisite image of Lakota lying before me in the air a few feet above the bed. It is not a dream. By now, the difference between a dream and a "visit" has become clear to me. "Visits," as I mentioned earlier, are like dreams that are in high definition. Not only are they much sharper—crystal clear, in fact—but the colors in them are so vibrant that there is just no confusing a dream with a contact, some of which come as I am falling asleep or waking up, as has occurred this morning. They also may include any of my senses. I have had visits in sight, sound, smell, and touch as well as visits in a sixth sense that I will describe as "knowing."

That evening, I find a photo of Lakota on the floor by the attic ladder. It is a picture of him that I particularly love, and normally keep in my room. In fact, I keep two of these pictures in my room...one in the book on my dresser and one in a book on my night table. I look, and they are both there where they always are. I have no idea where this third one, laying on the floor at the bottom of the stairs, came from.

I go into the living room, sit down, and—as is my habit on this night, once a week, before I settle in to relax for the evening—I take my blood pressure. As I go to remove the cuff from my wrist I am startled to see a bright red heart on the blood pressure cuff. I have used that cuff many, many times and never noticed it. So has Bill, and when I ask him, he says he never noticed it either. It's odd that both of us never noticed a bright red heart on a white background. Perhaps this is a coincidence, but I don't believe in coincidences—especially when preceded by a photograph that appears out of nowhere! It is also exactly three months today since Lakota crossed over. He is staying in close contact because he knows how badly I need it.

By far, the time I most often have contacts is when I am waking up from a light nap—usually in my recliner in front of the TV. Something gently awakens me. It is never jarring, but I am totally awake. Those are the times I get beautiful, visual images. Sometimes they are translucent. Occasionally they are solid. I am careful at these times to avoid moving my head. These images need to be viewed slightly to the side, so the rods in your eyes—cells that see faint images—are concentrated. If you turn and look straight at the image it will disappear because you will be looking with the cones—the cells that see color.

A chill ran through Donna and the hairs on her arms stood up. She had not heard that sound since her dad had departed.

CHAPTER TWENTY-FIVE:

Willow: Several Years Ago

In a previous chapter, I wrote about how I saw signs that Lakota's adopted brother, Zeak, came to "escort" Lakota when it was time for him to cross over the Rainbow Bridge. This is not the first time I have run across this idea of loved ones coming to help us when it is our time to leave the physical world. My mother started seeing her dog a few days before she passed. As noted earlier, a hospice nurse once told me she knew when people were going to pass within a few days, because they started getting "visits" from deceased loved ones. It doesn't seem to matter whether these "visitors" are humans or animals. What does seem to matter is the bond they had with the person who is departing.

Another story from trainer Donna Riley involves her father's dog: a beagle named "Willow." Donna's dad was a hunter, and he had hunting dogs for most of his life. Willow was the last dog he ever had. He bought the beagle to be his hunting dog. But he was getting on in years and was caring for his wife, who had heart problems and cancer, so he really didn't have the time or energy to hunt anymore. So, he would take Willow into the woods and run her and let her scent around and do what she was bred to do, so she would be a fulfilled, happy dog. For the rest of the time, she was his close companion.

Eventually Donna's father also developed cancer. Being a caretaker for his wife and being ill himself proved to be too much; it became too difficult for him to care for Willow, too. So Donna took Willow for him. This way the dog would get the care and exercise she needed, but Donna could bring Willow to visit her father, so he would get to see her, and her mom enjoyed seeing Willow, too.

During this time, Donna's parents mostly stayed in the house. Her dad only went out to take out the garbage. His route took him down the front porch steps, out of the house, and around a large bush, to where the garbage cans were kept. Then he took the garbage cans to the curb. After the trash was collected, he would follow this route in reverse.

Typical of a hunting beagle, Willow had a specific sound she made when she was scenting a trail. It was a cross between and bark and a howl. She would not make that sound for anything else, and after she stopped going hunting with her owner, she only made that sound for one thing: her owner.

Every time Donna took Willow to visit her parents, the dog practiced a ritual: She would walk with Donna to the front porch, start to make that specific tracking sound, and track the exact path Donna's dad took to take out and bring in the garbage. The little dog insisted on tracking her owner's path before going into the house to visit. When she entered the house, she would run around and find Donna's dad, and when she found him, she made that sound again. She would wag her tail happily to greet Donna's mother, but she did not make that sound. That sound was just for him, and him alone.

While she was living with Donna, Willow developed a cardiac issue called Dilated Cardiomyopathy (DCM), a disease of the heart muscle. Occasionally, this would cause her to pass out, and she was on medication for it. The attacks would come on suddenly, with no warning. Several times when it had happened, Donna had thought Willow was dead, and run over to her, only to have Willow get up and act like she was fine.

Time passed, and both of Donna's parents passed away, in close succession. Three years later, the following event happened:

Willow liked to sleep on a blanket on the floor of Donna's bedroom. That was her choice. She could have slept on the bed, but she preferred the floor. On one particular night, she jumped up on the bed, and from there, stepped onto a cedar chest that was under a window in the bedroom. Since Willow had never done this before, Donna was puzzled as to what the dog was doing, and turned on her night light to get a better view. To Donna's amazement, Willow was intently looking out the window, when she let out that special bark/howl sound that was only for Donna's dad. Three or four times, the loud bark/howling sound reverberated through the house. A chill ran through Donna and the hairs on her arms stood up. She had not heard that sound since her dad had departed.

Willow jumped off the bed, and Donna got up to settle the little dog down. Willow seemed fine, so Donna got back into bed. She heard Willow's paw make a noise, pulling open the door, which had been a little ajar, so she could go out into the hall. There was a fleece dog bed out there, and Willow got into it and settled down. Donna fell asleep.

Later that night, Donna got up to use the bathroom. She noticed Willow in the dog bed. When she turned on the light in the hall, she could immediately see that Willow had passed away. Normally, Donna would have been very emotional at the loss of a pet, but she never cried a tear, because she knew who had been at the window: Donna's dad had come to get his dog.

I reacted the minute I saw her,

because, O.M.G.,

she was a smaller version

of The Zeakie Dog!

CHAPTER TWENTY-SIX:

I Don't Ever Want Another Dog: July 22, 2016

In four more days it will be four months since my beloved Lakota left the physical world. The *Reader's Digest* condensed version of the experience is that it has been the worst pain I have ever suffered. I have survived by spending a lot of time processing his photos and creating several memorials to him. I have not been ready to even think about another dog. More than once I have told myself that I never want to go through this again, so I never, ever, ever wanted another dog. When I have had dogs visiting here, other than Cooper, I felt uncomfortable if they happened to lay down in one of the places where Lakota liked to lie. I knew it wouldn't be fair to another dog to subject him or her to this deep, sorrowful, energy.

As time went by I thought more about it. I didn't ever want to go through this again. On the other hand, I was miserable. I didn't even know who I was without a dog. I kept vacillating between missing having a dog in my life and being terrified at the thought of it. I realized that if I ever did get another dog, it would need to be a very different dog from Lakota, so I could keep my thoughts and feelings distinctly separated, in order to be fair to the new dog. I also decided that if I did get another dog, this time it would be a rescue. I had always raised my dogs from puppyhood. But if I were to ever get over this fear and decide to get another dog, I wanted to use the knowledge I had acquired over the years to help a dog that really needed it. And, because of my age, I wanted an adult dog. I didn't want to predecease my dog because my dogs bonded deeply with me, and I didn't want to put a dog through what I had gone through. I knew that it was harder to find homes for older dogs—especially ones with issues. I also had decided I wanted a dog around forty pounds because Bill and I were getting older, and it had been very difficult for us to help Lakota when he had mobility problems because he was a big boy at eighty-two pounds.

On Friday afternoon, July 22nd, as I was driving home from an appointment, my point of view suddenly flipped: I knew it was time, and I knew it was time RIGHT NOW! Driven by this deep, urgent feeling, I called all the local shelters, but it was late on a Friday afternoon and no one answered. I looked at pictures on internet rescue sites, but nothing stirred me, and I really needed to look at dogs in person to feel for a connection.

I called my friend Donna to see if she might know of a specific dog in that size range that one of her rescue contacts had. When I told her what I was feeling, she told me that there was probably a dog trying to find its way to me—a dog that was meant to be mine. As soon as she said the words, I knew she was right. I made a few more calls and finally found a facility—a branch of a top-notch, very well-known rescue organization—that had several medium-sized dogs available for adoption that I could look at right away. I told the woman that I had an exceptional home to offer a dog: a home with a dog door, a large, shady, securely fenced-in yard, off-leash hiking trails, a lake, and dog friends. I told her I was an experienced dog person and was willing to adopt an adult dog, because I was confident I could work with any problems that the dog might have. I told her that if I connected with a dog, I would want to bring him or her right home with me, so I offered her my vet's name and number and asked her to call ahead for a reference. Then Bill and I got in the car—all I brought was my wallet, a slip lead, and a copy of *Walking with the Shadow of Love* to show them where this dog would be living—and headed west to the facility.

About a half-hour later, we pulled into the adoption center. We went inside and walked to the rear of the building where we had been directed. When we reached the adoption desk, I asked the woman if she was Amanda—the woman I had spoken to—and she said that she was. As we talked, a dog in a glass room behind the desk immediately caught my eye and I felt a stirring in my gut—I told Amanda that I thought I saw MY dog. I reacted the minute I saw her because, O.M.G., she was a smaller version of The Zeakie Dog! I asked if I could interact with her, walk her, and introduce her to a strange person and a strange dog. The one thing I preferred to not deal with was an aggressive dog, because I didn't think it was fair to bring one into the community, so I needed to check her out. She assured me I could, and asked me to wait a minute while she brought the dog into the meet and greet room. She then came to get us.

She was beautiful and her resemblance to Zeak
with her striking black and white markings
and pretty, speckled boots
and paws really rattled me.

We walked in and sat down. "Run," as they had temporarily named her, looked like a flat-coated border collie and that's what the adoption center had her listed as. She was beautiful and her resemblance to Zeak, with her striking black and white markings and pretty, speckled boots and paws really rattled me. I especially liked that her long black tail had a white tip. I had admired that feature on a dog I often saw at the park, who had been friends with Lakota. For some reason, it had really appealed to me, and now here it was on this dog I was attracted to. Besides, it looked like a paintbrush...the perfect tail for an artist's dog!

When the dog came over, she seemed timid, so I ignored her and allowed her to sniff me and asked Bill to do the same. Amanda told me that the dog had just been moved there from their main facility that morning. She had refused to eat all day, and refused to play, even though they had her in a room full of toys. She was a stray and had been in their main facility for over a month being fed, chipped, vaccinated, flea and tick bathed and treated, parasite treated, spayed, operated on for a hernia, and allowed to heal. She had been in bad shape when she was brought in—filthy, with very dirty ears and long nails. Her weight: my exact dog target weight: forty pounds.

When we took a short walk outside, the dog pulled hard on the leash, to the point of choking herself. "I can work with this problem," I thought. Meetings with some volunteers in the store went well and "Run" approached them without incident. Amanda brought out another rescue dog, and we introduced them. They greeted each other calmly and politely. That, coupled with my strong feelings of attraction and connection to this dog, was enough for me. I told Amanda that I would like to adopt "Run." I knew that I would be renaming her soon. Before I signed the papers, Amanda told me that the dog had Lyme disease and gave me a prescription bottle of Doxycycline. I told her I was adopting this dog "for better or for worse."

We filled out the forms, paid the adoption fee, bought food and some other doggy items, and left to take "Run" home to begin her new life in a loving "forever" home. As we left, Amanda said, "When we spoke on the phone I was hoping you would adopt this dog, and I had a feeling you would. That's why I had her in the window. She deserves a break!" On the way home, I called Elaine and Allie and told them the news. They were very excited and asked when they could see our new family member. I told them I would love them to visit with Cooper when we got home because I thought that interacting with another dog who had such stable energy would help our new girl settle in.

When we got home, we went in the back gate. I teared up as I opened the gate and saw the sign that read, "Lakota and Zeak's Playground." I let "Run" off leash in her large, beautiful, grassy, new yard with the coyote-resistant fence, and she trotted around aimlessly until our neighbors arrived. She seemed to be unresponsive and in shock, having been moved twice in one day, and having gone through unknown trauma before she was picked up by the rescue organization. After a short visit, we allowed her to explore her new home and fixed her something to eat. Since she had refused to eat all day, I was relieved to see her gobble up her food.

We had just sat down in the living room to see if our new girl would play with her toys, when she abruptly shifted gears and went on a rampage of chewing/sucking on a fleece throw in the living room while grinding her teeth. In seconds, there were several large holes in the throw. She then proceeded to pee on the carpet several times in the space of a half-hour. She became very hyper and seemed to be having some kind of panic attack. I sat on the floor to see if she would come to me and if I could calm her. She came right over, but as I petted and massaged her she became even more excited, and soon was mouthing me up and down my arms. She wasn't doing it hard, but this was a five- or six-year-old dog acting like a puppy with no bite inhibition. That coupled with the blanket-sucking pointed to one of two things from my body of knowledge: Either she was taken from her mother too young, or she had been through trauma and was suffering from anxiety. It could be the shock of being abandoned, and then the additional stress of weeks of confinement, painful cleaning and medical treatments, and then being moved twice in one day from the only home she had known for over a month.

When it came time to go to bed, I went into my room to set up a crate for her. I am not a fan of crates, but I do believe a dog should be acclimated to a crate in case they have to be hospitalized. Since she had been in a rescue for over a month, I assumed she was crate-trained. I knew I couldn't leave her loose in the state she was in because she could chew through electrical wires or eat the couch! I put one of the fleece throws she had chewed holes in into the crate with a small bucket of water. As I was preparing the crate, she jumped on the bed, and before I could remove her, she chewed a hole in the fleece blanket on the bed! This sweet, placid dog from the rescue had turned into a one-dog house wrecker on some kind of rampage!

After successfully taking her out to relieve herself, I profusely praised her, gave her a bunch of treats, and put her into the crate—minus the fleece. She settled down, but as soon as I got into bed next to her crate, she started screaming at ear-shattering decibels! I knew I couldn't let her out while she was screaming because that would reinforce it, but I also couldn't let her loose in the house if she did calm down because of the fabric eating. I was concerned that all the fluff she was eating could cause an obstruction. She had also eaten the coating off of two tennis balls, so fast that I had no time to take them from her. I decided she would have to spend the night in the crate, and it was upsetting because I thought she might have been crate-abused (left in a crate most of the time by her original owners), or chained out all the time, and had developed the OCD chewing/sucking to cope. But I couldn't let her out because she could choke to death on ingested fabric, or bloat—a common name for a life-threatening condition called gastric dilation volvulus, or wind up with an intestinal obstruction. I had always raised my dogs from puppies and never had a dog with a behavior problem. However, I was pretty knowledgeable about dealing with them and felt it was time to pay my dues and help a difficult dog get a second chance. As I tried to fall asleep, I couldn't help thinking that this dog was lucky I rescued her, because in the hands of an inexperienced person, she might have gone right back to the shelter by now. Maybe she had before. Maybe these problems were why such a beautiful dog was in rescue. I was hopeful she could be helped and determined to be the one to do it; however both our new family member and I had a restless night with very little sleep.

After Lakota passed, I kept getting images of a pink baby carriage when I meditated. I did not know I would be getting another dog at the time, in fact I was convinced I would not. But those feelings suddenly changed, and when I did get my next dog, it was a female. About a month before the pandemic hit, Zeak sent me an image of a person in a hazmat suit. It made no sense at the time. After the pandemic made the news, it made perfect sense. Sometimes our animals are ahead of what is coming. The images they send may not make sense at the time, but later they do.

Our new family member drew a small group of admirers at the park---
she really was quite beautiful.

CHAPTER TWENTY-SEVEN:

The Morning After: July 23, 2016

Morning arrived and I dragged my sleep-deprived body out of bed, opened the door to our new family member's crate, blocked her charging out and made her calm down first, and took her out immediately to relieve herself. I made our respective breakfasts, gave her a couple of different scented chew toys, and went about the business of the morning, keeping one eye on "Run." I knew we would be meeting our dog-walking friends at 10:00 a.m., as we did every morning, and that would be the best medicine for our girl. I also knew she would have to stay on a leash for quite some time until she could be off-leash trained and reliable.

Our new family member drew a small group of admirers at the park—she really was quite beautiful. She was nervous and hesitant and still too much in shock to enjoy this inviting walk in the woods. She was awful on the leash, and my arms ached from her pulling. I needed to teach this dog how to walk properly as soon as possible.

One of the things that caused her the most anxiety was the car—or rather, the car door. She panicked every time the door opened. If she was outside the car and I opened the door, she was so desperate to get in the car she almost climbed up my leg! It reinforced my theory that the way she was abandoned was by being pushed out a car door. We had switched to walking at a nearby park with wider trails because it was safer and she screamed and cried all the way during the seven-minute drive to and from the park every day. I ignored it, and anytime it got quiet for a few seconds, quickly gave her a treat and praised her. After making her sit and calm down before getting in the car many, many times for months, with treats for rewards, she began to lose her car anxiety.

I had decided to use umbilical training for this dog, since I couldn't let her out of my sight anyway. This is a type of training where you tie the dog to you all the time. It helps calm dogs with anxiety and it also helps to form a bond quickly. It was a method used by a group of monks who were known for having really balanced, obedient, well-adjusted dogs. I used a seven-foot, two-ended tether leash. Please note that I would never tether a dog to an object or outside. It is dangerous to the dog's safety and can cause all sorts of behavior problems. Tied-out dogs are sitting ducks for predators such as coyotes, are helpless against biting and stinging insects, and can get hung on their tie-outs.

My plan for my new dog was: obedience training, one forty-five-minute walk and one hard play session a day, and implementing N.I.L.I.F. (Nothing in Life is Free)—a training method where the dog has to earn everything, even if only by a simple sit. What I found surprising was that a five- or six-year-old dog had zero training and didn't even know what "sit" meant. I worked with her on "sit" and "come," and also her learning to use the dog door. For this, I enlisted the help of Cooper, who knew well how to use the door—seeing him go through the door greatly increased "Run's" motivation to do it. One would never know this, however, because she relieved herself on the carpet no less than six times during the day—another sign that she was in a crate or chained outdoors most of the time. I was confident that all of this would resolve, once she had time to adjust to her awesome new life…she just couldn't believe in it—or me—yet after what she had been through. How does anything—or anyone—trust after being neglected, abused, and abandoned?

The next important task I needed to tend to was giving her a name. I believe the name we give our dogs carries energy with it that affects who they become, so I would choose carefully. I wanted a Native American name—I explain the reason for this in *Walking with the Shadow of Love*—and I also wanted to like the sound of the name. After scanning lists on the internet, I chose a Hopi name: "Kaya." It meant "elder sister." I liked it because of her being an adult when I adopted her, and also because I am an elder sister, too. I told Kaya her new name, gave her a massage, and even though it had taken her three days to learn to "sit" reliably, she learned her name and responded to it almost instantly. This was surprising…almost as though she knew it was to be her name.

After the first night, I was aware the crate was just too traumatic for her. It would take a long time to condition her to it without stressing her, and she might have what is called containment anxiety, and never be able to be crated. So I got her a bed, placed it on the floor next to my bed, and had her get in and lie down.

She loved it! I think she was shocked to have something of her own that was soft to sleep on. When she tried to latch on to it to chew/suck on, I said, "no" and she stopped and never tried again.

However, as much as she liked the bed, she wanted to sleep with me! After calmly but decisively removing her from my bed twenty or more times, she finally got the message that she had to sleep in her bed. I was near collapse from the effort. My long-term goal was for her to be my bed-buddy, but it was way too soon to allow that yet. She needed discipline very badly because that was what would calm her and give her confidence. It was not a good night's sleep for me again, but by morning she was settled in her place.

I noticed how grateful she seemed to be for everything she received from me. Not only for the bed, but for toys, treats, food, and anything I gave her. Dogs understand gifts. A friend and former classmate that I sing with occasionally told me a great story about his rescue dog and a gift. Every day when they took their morning walk, he and his dog passed this old Labrador tied out in his yard. One morning my friend's dog insisted on bringing his rawhide chip along on their walk. My friend tried to discourage it at first, but then became curious why the dog wanted to bring it, so he let him. When they reached the old Labrador's house, the old dog was not out. My friend's dog went into the old dog's yard, left the chip where the dog was tied out, and urinated next to, but not on, the chip. He left the old dog a gift and signed a greeting card to go with it!

The next day, after Kaya's morning walk, we took her to our vet. We wanted her generally checked over.

She was coughing, which had started after the chewing and eating of part of three fleece throws, and also chewing the covers off of two tennis balls. Our vet said Kaya was very anxious—so much so that her heart was racing to a concerning degree—and had irritated her trachea ingesting and possibly inhaling some of the fleece and tennis ball covering. This was also concerning, she said, because Kaya had a collapsing trachea. This may have been the result of abuse, because, while it is a birth defect in some in small dogs, it is uncommon in a dog this large. It can be the result of harsh jerking on a dog's neck from chain collars to the point that it crushes the cartilage that holds the dog's breathing opening open. Whenever the dog breathes in quickly or forcefully, such as when it is excited or exercising, the opening closes and the dog cannot get air. The effect is similar to sucking a thick milkshake too hard through a paper straw. Surgical corrections for this condition are often problematic. A chronic cough often accompanies the condition, and the more the dog coughs, the worse the condition gets. Once we were told Kaya had this condition, we switched her to a halter, because she should not have a collar around her neck.

Kaya's teeth were somewhat worn down from her tooth grinding. Other than that and the Lyme, she was doing OK. Dr. Rao prescribed a steroid for the throat irritation and a plug-in that emitted an undetectable pheromone scent that a mother dog makes when she nurses her pups. This would help her—and therefore me—to sleep at night. Mercifully, it worked, and we both got our first good night's sleep!

Kaya and I stayed attached to one another for weeks. Every morning we went hiking on the trails for forty-five minutes to an hour. At night I disconnected us, but she slept beside me in her bed. Because she was tied to me all day, it meant that I was there to comfort her all the time as she faced all of the "firsts" in her new life. I was able to provide calm leadership when she was frightened and affection when she was calm. During this period of time I did basic obedience training for five minutes every morning and evening with lots of tiny treats as rewards.

As I spent time with Kaya, I began to piece together some of her story. One night my husband was heading into his room to change and started taking his belt off as he walked across the living room. As soon as he started to remove the belt, Kaya went ballistic: frantically barking, hackles up, and lunging and then backing off repeatedly. It was clear that something had been done to her by a man taking his belt off. She also got very upset if Bill went to sit in his recliner.

Another thing about her was quite surprising. I think she was tied out and lonely and her only friend was a cat. Kaya is the most catlike dog I have ever seen. She pounces on toys like a cat, makes cat-like sounds, and purrs like a cat if she is very relaxed and enjoying a belly rub. She even has a marking on her shoulder that looks like a cat!

From the beginning, although I did have my moments of doubt, I believed that Kaya's issues would yield to consistent training, exercise, and love. What I wasn't expecting was how much the umbilical training accelerated the whole process. After a week she was so bonded to me it was touching. She stopped peeing in the house after the third day, stopped chewing and eating our things, and transferred her chewing to chew toys after a few days, and even learned that tennis balls were for fetching—not chewing. We were starting to leave her home alone for very short periods of time. At my vet's urging, I left and came right back several times a day, going in and out different doors, to desensitize her to the sound of my keys and my purse. I also picked up my keys and purse and just went into other rooms.

Kaya had never been taught any obedience commands. I made sure I was consistent with my words, actions, and rewards. One exception to the tethering was when, every afternoon, I took Kaya out into our long, fenced-in yard. I gave my husband a handful of treats and I took a handful too. He went to the far end of the yard. I took Kaya off the tether for a few minutes and we took turns calling her and rewarding her when she came. She loved and needed the hard running. We also played some fetch with her to be sure she got in enough running to drain her energy.

But the biggest joy of all came when I had the confidence in our bond to turn her loose to run with the other dogs. Kaya by now was calmer, she made wonderful eye contact with me and paid attention when I talked, and had great recall in the back yard. When we speak of recall in dog training, we mean that the dog responds and comes to you immediately when you call them. It is probably the most important command you can teach your dog. On the day I decided would be the day, we walked with Elaine and Cooper, so we had an "anchor dog" with us. I made sure Kaya knew I had a pocket full of treats, discretely removed the tether so Kaya didn't really notice, and started confidently walking down the trail. I pictured her walking along with me, and that is exactly what she did. I don't know if she had ever been given that trust before, because at first she stayed right next to me. I gestured to her and told her it was "OK," her release word. Her eyes lit up when she realized I was telling her she could go sniff and explore, and then...*JOY!* She ran and sniffed and got to be a dog! Every time I called her in, she spun around and flew to me. It was a beautiful sight to see her jumping over fallen trees in her haste to come back to me. As time went by, I learned that she came to me even if she saw a stranger coming down the trail. And even more amazing, she came to me even if that stranger was a dog! So the time and effort, love and patience I invested in her resulted in a dog that I could trust.

Kaya was reliable and responsive off-leash. If she saw a squirrel and started to chase it, she stopped instantly when I called her in. Our bond was now stronger than her prey drive and stronger than her fear.

I still cried tears for Lakota. I still ached for him. I still felt him and sensed his presence. But Kaya was helping me heal because I waited until I knew I was ready. And I was helping her heal because she was courageous enough to begin to trust again, despite having her share of good reasons to not trust humans. But she is not all the way there with me yet, and she does not trust other humans at all. That is going to take a lot of love and a lot of cookies!

Grooming was also quite a process. It took a while and a lot of patience, starting off in tiny increments, but she now lets me grind her nails, brush her teeth with an electric toothbrush, and—this was the most difficult of all—lets me clean her ears. The first time I gently tried to wipe out her ears with an ear wipe, she screamed so loud I took her to the vet. I thought she must have had an ear infection. There was nothing wrong. Her medical records from the rescue had a comment on how dirty her ears had been. I suspect cleaning them must have hurt her. All three of these procedures terrified her at first. I never forced the issue—I was gently persistent, always asking her to lie down and gradually submit, but never forcing her or holding her down. And, of course, I always had tiny treats on hand to instantly reward good behavior.

Once in a while, mostly in the car, she still panics. But for most of the time, she is a lovely, well-behaved, model dog. She has come farther, faster that any human who had been through what she has could have. Rescuing her has been one of the most rewarding things I have ever done. I am frequently touched by how brave she is about trusting me with things that are really frightening to her. I truly feel honored at these times. She gives me love, loyalty, fun, and brings her beauty into my world every day. People we meet say how lucky they think she is, but in truth, it is I who am the lucky one!

I could not take my eyes off of her for a minute.

CHAPTER TWENTY-EIGHT:

Trust: July 2016

Trust is one of the most fragile things on earth. Whether you are dealing with an abused or abandoned human or animal, it is a huge issue. I believe that trust is the foundation of any relationship. Even one lie can destroy it. Some of us extend our trust pretty generously and some of us are very cautious; and our decision as to which of these attitudes we adopt is usually based on past experience.

If we are a human, it begins in childhood. If we are blessed with parents who make an effort to keep their word—do the things they say they will do and not do the things they say they won't—we develop the ability to trust. When we get older, the same process takes place with friends and partners. If we are fortunate and smart enough—it takes both luck and good judgment—to surround ourselves with people who are honorable, we develop trusting relationships with our friends and partners. If trust is broken enough times by any of these people along the way, our ability to trust is damaged.

The same is true of our animals. Until I rescued Kaya, I had raised all of my dogs from puppies. Yes,

I adopted The Zeakie Dog (actually, he adopted me), but I did so when he was still a puppy. My dogs Cinder, Santana, Lakota, and Zeak all learned that I meant and did what I said. They knew they would always be taken care of. They knew if I told them something was OK, it wasn't going to hurt. They knew they were loved. Because of these things, they trusted me. I believe that trust is required to keep the heart open, and when it is betrayed, the heart closes to protect itself, whether that heart belongs to a human or a rescue dog named Kaya.

Kaya's damage included: anxiety, panic attacks, OCD, fabric sucking/eating, tooth grinding, and excessive licking syndrome…sometimes to the point of self-mutilation. For the first few days she was with us she was chewing and destroying things, getting into wastebaskets and chewing up the contents, and counter surfing…a term used to describe dogs stealing food off of countertops. I could not take my eyes off of her for a minute.

If I had to guess how Kaya wound up in the streets—if I tried to piece together what happened to get her there, from her behavior—her story would go like this:

A busy family with kids, on impulse, buys a cute puppy in a pet store. Appearance and cuteness are all they are concerned about. They have no interest in determining if the puppy is a breed suitable to their lifestyle. The puppy is from a puppy mill. She has been separated from her abused, malnourished mother and siblings when she is too young. The family who buys the dog knows nothing about dogs, and they don't bother to educate themselves before they go ahead and get one, so they buy a high-energy breed that needs a lot of exercise because *they like the way it looks*. They have no time for walks, no time to train a dog, and no idea how to do it if they did have time, so they go to work and ignore it. When they come home they come home to a mess—a young puppy can only hold it for a half hour, and shouldn't be asked to do more—and stuff damaged by the puppy because it is bored and lonely.

As the puppy develops its normal sharp, first teeth, it starts nipping everybody, partly because the puppy mill took it from its mother and siblings too soon and it never learned bite inhibition, and partly because it is teething. This is perfectly normal behavior for very young dogs. When it nips the kids they scream and yell, which makes the puppy even more agitated, and no one teaches them the proper way to behave around an animal. This creates an even more out-of-control puppy. It's not fun anymore. So the parents stuff the puppy in a crate or chain it outside all the time. This is a recipe for madness. The intelligent, high-energy puppy is going out of its mind from not being able to work off its energy and having no mental activity. Over a few years' time, the dog's frustration develops into Obsessive Compulsive Disorder, sucking on fabric and toys and grinding its teeth. It cries and screams to be let out of its prison. It is occasionally beaten by its annoyed humans and has its choke collar jerked so hard that it breaks her trachea.

Eventually, Dad and/or Mom, having decided they have had enough, hatch a plan. They don't want to drop the dog off at a shelter because they don't want to admit the truth: That they are getting rid of the dog because they don't want to provide the proper care for it—it is an inconvenience. Dad or Mom waits till the kids are in bed, goes into the bedroom where the dog is sleeping, picks it up, and takes it out to the car. He or she puts it in the car and drives it far, far away. Then he/she stops the car in a dark place, shoves the dog out of the car, and speeds off. Done. And that is the story of the day trust died.

One evening, just after Kaya and I went to bed, we were hit by a fierce thunderstorm. It was the first one we had since we adopted Kaya. When the first loud clap of thunder hit, a terrified Kaya got out of her bed and came to the edge of mine. She stood on her hind legs, shaking in terror, her eyes pleading with me to let her up on the bed with me. I decided it was time to do that. If Kaya couldn't turn to me for comfort when she was frightened, how could she trust me.

She snuggled next to me and close as she could get. She was still trembling. I talked to her in a soothing voice and stroked her gently. As I did so I felt a shift. It happened so quickly that I was taken aback, and in that moment, Kaya and I deeply bonded, this time on a spiritual level. There would be many times ahead when I would be dazzled by how brave she was, but perhaps the bravest thing she ever did was to open her heart to me after what humans had done to her. I felt a deep, powerful wave of love wash over us. From then on, we were so close that I could barely tell where I ended, and Kaya began.

But there was something intriguing about them:
one looked like Carney,
and the other looked like Van Gogh,
but with some white markings.

CHAPTER TWENTY-NINE:

The Déjà Vu Cats: November 3, 2017

My friend Cathy and I go back to 1967, when we became sisters-in-law. We later became ex-sisters-in-law, but have remained friends for all the years since. Like many of my friends, she has had her own experiences with the spirit world. One of them involved a cat whom she gave her family name: Carney.

Carney came into Cathy's life when her daughter, Sheryl, saw a litter of kittens in a supermarket parking lot, which the owner was trying to find homes for. The owner had several small children who were handling the kittens roughly and inappropriately, and Sheryl took two of them just to get them away from the bad situation they were in. Sheryl kept one and named it Van Gogh, and Cathy kept the other one and named it Carney.

Carney was Cathy's companion for twenty and a half years, a good, long, life for a cat. He had survived two operations, both for a sarcoma caused by a rabies shot. But even good, long lives eventually end. Carney's time here in the physical world finally ran out—right at home, on November 3, 2017. Of course it was a hard loss for Cathy. And like many of us after a loss, she just wasn't ready to decide what to do with Carney's belongings. She concentrated on giving her other cat, Kyla, some extra attention to help them both heal, and lost track of where she put Carney's things.

On December 3, 2017—exactly one month to the day after Carney's passing, Cathy got a call from her daughter, Sheryl, who lived about a half-hour away. Sheryl's cat, Van Gogh, had died a few years earlier. Sheryl had called to tell Cathy that she had rescued two kittens from a red-tailed hawk. The mother of the kittens was nowhere around and the hawk was after the babies, so Sheryl had brought them inside because she couldn't leave them. She was going to raise them herself and, when they were old enough, find homes for them. But there was something intriguing about them: one looked like Carney, and the other looked like Van Gogh. Prodded by the coincidence, Cathy and Sheryl each adopted the cat that resembled their departed cat. Cathy's adoption went through the usual adjustment period of the new cat, whom she named Finnegan, and her other cat, Kyla, acclimating to each other, but all went well.

Like a lot of the houses near our lake, Cathy's house had a loft. The loft was used, much like an attic, for storage, and there was a lot of stuff up there. It wasn't unusual for one or both of the cats to go up there. But on one particular afternoon, as Cathy was sitting in the living room, the new cat—Carney's lookalike—went up to the loft, exploring. After he investigated for a while, the cat walked to the edge of the loft with something in his mouth, something that he had found and picked up out of all of the things up there. Then he positioned himself, carefully dropped the object off the edge of the loft right onto Cathy's lap.

Cathy jumped, startled by the object falling from the loft and hitting her lap. She did a double-take when she saw what it was. It was Carney's collar.

In Kaya's case, I believe obedience training saved her from insanity. It taught her how to calm and control herself.

CHAPTER THIRTY:

Perseverance: August 2016

It never ceases to amaze me how powerful basic obedience training is. Kaya had a myriad of behavior issues when we brought her home. I have only actually addressed a few of them. The rest of them simply disappeared as she began to learn the rules and accept me as the person in charge. She is still a work in progress. By far the most difficult task has been getting her to walk at my side with a loose leash consistently. She does it beautifully some of the time. We are still working on getting her to do it all of the time. By all of the time I mean even if an ill-behaved, out-of-control dog is dragging its owner down the trail towards us while yelping, lunging, and screaming at us! Often these dogs are on retractable leashes which, in my opinion, actually teach dogs to pull. This occurs because these leashes put constant tension on the dog's neck, desensitizing it to the tension of their pulling. This is exactly what you don't want if you ever want your dog to walk calmly on a loose leash. These leashes have amputated dog's legs and people's fingers. Also, your dog should not be so far away from you—you won't have time to pull them back if a car comes around a bend. Lastly, having your dog out in front of you puts it in a protective, defensive mode and it is more likely to become leash-reactive. I will explain leash-reactive in another chapter when I have to deal with it with Kaya.

The second issue—which we have made great progress with—is anxiety. Basic obedience training, a consistent schedule, and rewarding calmness have really helped Kaya to relax. I also use "relax" as a command, and when I observe her in a very calm state I say, "good relax," and give her a treat. Another powerful tactic is waiting—waiting for her to sit and calm down before she gets in the car, is fed, is allowed to greet another dog, or is allowed to greet another person.

The third issue we are working on is the "stay" command. Because Kaya is an energetic herding dog, it is hard for her to stay put for any length of time, especially if there are distractions. So we continue to work on this one.

The fourth issue with Kaya is food hysteria. (I also suffer from this, especially around chocolate!) She sits quietly and patiently at the entrance to the kitchen—where she has been told to wait—while I prepare her meals, because she doesn't get fed until she does. Kaya also knows she has to sit quietly before I give her a treat. However, she gets bold and insistent with other people who have treats. This can be difficult to control because once or twice people have given her treats at the *wrong time*: when she is half off the ground or actively begging. One incorrect move like that by another person can ruin weeks of training and create a lot of work getting a dog back to good behavior, especially when training an untrained adult dog. Some people don't care if their dogs act that way. I do and they should!

Here's why it is important to insist on proper manners from your dog: Most of the time, dogs who hurt people or other dogs begin with simple transgressions in basic manners. A dog pulling its human down the street is not going to listen very well in other situations. A dog allowed to jump for treats can really hurt someone. Sometimes owners of small dogs don't mind behavior like this because the injury potential is limited; but if they don't enforce the rules with other people's dogs that are larger, it can create problems for them. For that reason, small dogs can start dogfights. And even a small dog can injure a toddler by jumping on them, and it also creates disrespect for small children that can lead to other issues. I have seen a dog's penchant for jumping on small children morph into mounting them—for some reason children's parents object to this type of behavior!

All of these little things can contribute to a dog being a nuisance and even lead to dominant behavior that becomes dangerous. Such things as allowing a dog to control the walk with pulling, not asserting your authority during feeding time, and allowing a dog to become possessive and "guard" toys and chews can escalate to growling, and then to biting. Allowing a dog to chase small animals can reinforce their prey drive. Then one day a small child is running and screaming in the yard and a formerly nice dog goes into prey mode and chases and bites the child. The owners say they are stunned and that their dog has never done anything like that before. But it *has*—just with chipmunks instead of a child. To that dog, a screaming, small being has always been prey. This serious transgression didn't have to happen. It is just one example of bad manners turning really serious.

One of my proudest moments with Lakota was watching him play with a friend's tiny little kindergartener. She had his ball, and was throwing it for him to fetch. Each time, he ran after it like a maniac, brought it back to her, calmed himself as he neared her, and gently put the ball on the ground in front of her. Time after time as she bent over and picked it up, I watched as my beautiful, powerful, eighty-two-pound dog respected the authority of this little girl, allowed her to take his ball without question, and didn't try to jump on her or take it before she threw it. It brought tears to my eyes, because Lakota would run through a brick wall to get a moving ball! Yet he had that self-control, respect, and gentleness with a little girl. This did not happen by itself. Yet I know there are a few people who think I am nit-picking because I insist on my dogs having good manners.

Since, with Kaya, I was working with an adult rescue with no previous training, teaching her took a little longer and required persistence. Lakota and Zeak were dogs I could take anywhere. They were rocks I could lean on and trust to be gentle and respectful with children. (Even with that, no dog should be left with children unsupervised. Sometimes, children are not gentle and respectful with dogs, and they may not know how to behave around animals!)

I remember the social worker at a hospital where Lakota and Zeak worked as therapy dogs telling me that she could trust them with fragile patients more than some small dogs who had been brought to visit, dogs that had jumped on patients who had surgical wounds and hurt them. Not all dogs are going to be therapy dogs, but all dogs have the potential to be around family members who have injuries or surgery—or around babies. Even a small dog can hurt if it jumps on an incision. One fine day, that cute little dog you think is funny when it growls at you when you take its toy can bite someone. And even a little dog can inflict a nasty wound on a small child.

It is SO worth the time you spend with a dog to teach it proper manners, and there is no reason training can't be fun for both you and your dog. In fact, it should be! It is also really worthwhile to go to an obedience class, so your dog learns to behave with other dogs around. Even five minutes of active training a day, followed by everyone in the household enforcing the rules during the rest of the day, can create a pleasant, polite, four-legged family member who is a joy to be around. *Marley and Me* may be fun to watch on a movie screen, but in reality, it is *not* fun to live with a dog like that—for you or anyone your dog comes in contact with.

In Kaya's case, I believe obedience training saved her from insanity. It taught her how to calm and control herself. That, in turn, helped her to calm her anxiety, and calming her anxiety helped prevent her from slipping into OCD, tooth grinding, and fabric sucking. The bottom line is that a lack of discipline doesn't help either dogs or kids. It takes perseverance to outlast a kid, waiting for good behavior. It takes A LOT of perseverance to outlast a dog!

Shy-Ann had such a range of emotions.
She was such a fierce warrior-watchdog,
but also was funny, playful,
and so very affectionate.

CHAPTER THIRTY-ONE:

Shy's Departure: August 21, 2016

It had been a brutally hot, humid, buggy summer. People from places like Arizona like to say about their hot days that it's a dry heat, so it doesn't bother you that much. That is not usually the case in New Jersey. When it's hot, it's also humid, and—yes—it does bother you…a lot. It was on a particularly hot day, late in the afternoon, when we received a phone call from my son. As soon as I heard his voice, I knew it wasn't good news.

He had called to tell me that a few hours earlier a bear had entered their yard. They were all outside at the time and didn't notice the bear till they heard Shy sound the alarm. They turned around to see her doing her job…the job she had been brought into their lives to do. The fact that Shy was a small Dobie had never mattered, because she had intense, powerful energy. She went after the bear with a vengeance and a fury that convinced the bear that he really wanted to be somewhere else in a hurry. He took off with Shy in hot pursuit. Tom called her back but it was too late. She aborted her chase of the bear and was on her way back…when she suddenly stopped and dropped to the ground. Tom ran to her and knelt down beside her. She was crying softly. This lasted about a minute and then she was gone. No vets. No drugs. No lingering old-age health problems—just gone. The bear had never touched her. It was her heart that had given out in the excitement and the heat.

When someone—human or beloved pet—passes like that, it is really rough on those they leave behind. They are stunned. They didn't see it coming. There is no time for the emotional preparation we go through when we know someone we love has a limited amount of time left here in the physical world. So even though Shy-Ann had lived a very long life—longer than most Dobies—my kids were devastated.

I'm going to go out on a limb here, but I am guessing that if Shy had been allowed to choose the way she left this world, this is exactly the way she would have chosen to go out. She would have been proud to be doing her job—to go out in the line of duty—because she was so dedicated to protecting her family. She extended that guardianship to our family when she was with us, as did Lakota and Zeak, and I always felt very safe when my grandson and I went hiking with the three of them. I didn't even worry about them being attacked because they projected such strong, confident energy that most animals would not have approached them. And I knew that if they encountered humans—even small children—they would be polite and gentle.

Shy-Ann had such a range of emotions. She was such a fierce warrior-watchdog, but also was funny, playful, and so very affectionate. Her favorite position around her people was submissive, rolled over on her back with her belly up in the air, begging for a tummy rub. If you tried to stop because your hand was getting tired of rubbing, she would nudge you with her nose to get you to do it more.

I remembered an incident a few years back when we had invited an elderly neighbor to one of our dog parties. When he arrived at our gate I walked over to open it for him and to keep the dogs from getting out. He saw Shy and quickly changed his mind about attending. He said he was afraid of the "vicious Doberman." I assured him that Shy would be gentle, friendly, and polite, and probably be on his lap cuddling within minutes if he sat on the couch. It took more than a little urging, before he—very tentatively—came in.

The party was a dog costume party—the theme was "dog prom"—and I took Shy into my room to put her princess costume on her. Among her personality quirks was the fact that she was a girly-girl. She loved "pawdicures" and any kind of grooming attention. Shy also loved to wear clothes, and her pink princess outfit was her favorite. It had a pink tutu, little puffy things that fit on her legs, and—yes—a tiara. I put her outfit on her and out into the living room she trotted. She headed right for the couch where our elderly, somewhat terrified neighbor was sitting. She jumped up next to him and softly lay down on his lap upside down, waiting to be told how pretty she looked, and wondering when her belly rub was going to happen.

Our neighbor looked stunned. "I can't believe I'm sitting here with a vicious Doberman on my lap...much less one with a pink tutu, who isn't attacking me!" He finally started rubbing her tummy and that was that—they were there for the better part of an hour and our neighbor was just one more person who had fallen in love with Shy.

If we took Shy to a dog park, she was the social butterfly of the place. She went to every person there, said a polite, friendly hello, and then leaned up against each and every one of them so they felt obliged to pet her. She also played with each and every dog, frequently play-bowing to telegraph her friendly intentions, and once they knew she meant no harm she played with those who could handle it, because she played fast, rough, and hard!

One of our Christmas dog parties was marked by the attendance of a new dog, a Havanese puppy named Charlie. Havanese are a small, extremely furry, Cuban breed of dog that has gained some popularity in the U.S. recently. As I mentioned earlier, Shy gave a "puppy pass" to young dogs. While she played rough with the older dogs, what she put up with and allowed a puppy to do to her was surprising. She romped and played gently with the furry little pup, allowing him to jump all over her, nip at her, bark at her, and pretty much do anything he wanted without calling him out on any of it. The two of them had eyes only for each other. None of us had ever seen anything quite like this lovefest! It went on for so long that I had to put a stop to it to let her take a break and rest, because she was getting up there in years and I could see she was getting tired.

We had so many wonderful times with Shy and now she was crossing over too. The only one left of our original core pack of dogs was Cooper. He was the last man standing. He had grieved the loss of his two brothers-in-spirit and now he would not see Shy anymore…at least not in a physical form. I do believe Lakota and Zeak visit him regularly as they do me. Elaine has suspected it, as evidenced by certain behaviors she has seen Cooper engaging in. But that doesn't stop us from missing those we love when they leave the physical world. And our animal friends are no different—they grieve and they suffer loss.

Cooper's relationship with Kaya was more like his relationship with Shy than any other. He found her exciting and interesting, but he was getting old and couldn't tear around much with Kaya, like he could with Lakota and Zeak and Shy. But every once in a while, he would get a glint of mischief in his eye, and a shot of adrenaline, and he would start jumping straight up and down, and then take off with a surprising burst of speed. Kaya would follow in hot herding-dog pursuit and they would have a great romp. Then I would have to intervene and call Kaya in before it was too much for Cooper. At least, Kaya was a good diversion for him and they could hang out peacefully together at my house, which was nice for both of them.

All of these thoughts passed by like a flowing stream while I sat processing Shy's passing. As I pondered it all, I saw my life as measured in dogs. Each one was its own era.

She would have been proud
to be doing her job---
to go out in the line of duty---
because she was so dedicated
to protecting her family.

This is a simulation of what the afterimage of Lakota lying on his mat looked like.

CHAPTER THIRTY-TWO:

The Afterimage: August 30, 2016

Since November 13, 2011, I have had enough contacts from Zeak and Lakota to fill several journals. Every time I have a visual contact, I always wonder if they are sending me these images as pictures in my mind, or if they are actually visually present and my eyes are really seeing them. On this particular night, I was about to get an answer.

I was in my usual nighttime location: watching TV in my recliner. To my right was the place we had put Lakota's cooling mat, which he lay on every night his last two months, because it eased his pain. As I was searching the DVR to see what I had recorded to watch, something caught my eye to my right and down—exactly in that spot where Lakota's mat had been. To my delight, it was a full, solid, visual image of Lakota. It lasted longer than most of the visual visits I have had, but something happened at the end of it that answered my question about these contacts. As Lakota's black image disappeared, it was replaced by a white afterimage. Its appearance surprised me, but when I realized its significance, I was very excited.

I had studied these visual images in my art classes in college. It was thought that when certain cells in the eyes were saturated with colors or black or white, the cells' sensitiv-

ity to those colors would be fatigued in some way, causing them to produce a negative afterimage. I remember seeing a demonstration of a green, black, and yellow American flag. We were told to stare at it for a minute and then to stare at a blank piece of paper. When we did, we saw a red, white, and blue American flag as an afterimage. We were all quite impressed by the demonstration.

According to the Encyclopaedia Britannica, *the definition of afterimage is as follows: "Afterimage, visual illusion in which retinal impressions persist after the removal of the stimulus, believed to be caused by the continued activation of the visual system. The afterimage may be positive, corresponding in colour or brightness to the original image, or negative, being less bright or of colours complementary to the original…"*

These visits I was receiving, in which I was seeing my dogs—and a few humans who had passed—were being seen by my eyes, and my eyes were reacting to this particular one, because it was there long enough, to create a negative afterimage.

This visit will always be one of my favorites, because it let me know that the spirits of my beloved pets were actually here in the room with me…not merely in my mind's eye.

My dog, who was just learning to trust, had once again had her trust betrayed.

CHAPTER THIRTY-THREE:

The Attack: September 2016

It was a Saturday morning and we were headed to the trails to walk. On Saturdays, we walked with a pack consisting of Elaine and Cooper and some other neighbors and their dogs. We had walked with this group since the days of Lakota and The Zeakie Dog, so the Saturday walk had become a tradition.

One of the dogs in the group was a large, mixed breed named Lucy, who was an insecure, unstable, somewhat fearful dog under certain circumstances. Once or twice she had gotten into scuffles with Zeak or Lakota, but they were powerful, confident dogs who made it clear they were not intimidated and could easily hold their own, and it had not happened again. This particular dog had also been around Shy on quite a few occasions and they had a lot of fun playing together, but the dog knew better than to mess with Shy. I had noticed that Lucy had a tendency to growl when she greeted unknown dogs, but I wrote it off as a type of greeting sound that some dogs make which one of my trainers had told me about.

There was no doubt that Lucy was a handful—sometimes her owners could not hold onto her on a leash. She had slammed into my knees more than once, run into me, sending me flying into a thorn bush, injuring my ankle and knee, and also seriously injured one of our neighbors—not deliberately, but because of the hyper, uncontrolled energy she exhibited. I considered the dog a danger to my aging knees, but did not take its behavior towards other dogs seriously enough, probably because I allowed myself to be influenced by the fact that I liked the dog's owner. Looking back on it, I think I was in some denial about it and I was about to seriously regret this.

As we started up the trail on this particular morning we all unleashed our dogs. Kaya had only walked with this dog a few times, but there had been no issues. This was one of Kaya's first few times off-leash and she was loving the smells and the company of her people and some other dogs. She was very obedient and had fabulous recall, which I had worked hard to instill in her before I allowed her to be off leash. As we climbed the first steep hill on the trail, Lucy pulled ahead of our pack. She was quite a bit ahead of us when Kaya decided to try to catch up to her. She broke into a trot and barked and moved out a little ahead of us.

Lucy had never liked dogs catching up to her or passing her. Lakota had tremendous sprinting speed and could catch her and pass her, and when he did, Lucy would bark and bark and run for all she was worth till Lakota ran out of gas and she could pass him. I knew that she didn't want anyone passing her, but it never occurred to me that she would do what happened next.

As Kaya drew closer, Lucy wheeled around and attacked her. Poor Kaya was barely half Lucy's size and didn't stand a chance. Lucy flipped Kaya over on her back and appeared ready to gut her. I ran over as fast as I could and used my hiking pole, my body, and my voice—which Lucy had responded to for years, thankfully—to pry her off of Kaya. One of the men in the group helped and tried to grab Lucy's collar, a brave but dangerous endeavor. He was lucky he didn't get bitten for his trouble. Dogs in an aggressive state can transfer the aggression to another dog, another person, or even their owner. As soon as I was able to get Lucy off of Kaya, Kaya ran away—screaming and terrified in full-blown flight.

Since she was a rescue with terrible anxiety in a new home, I feared she would never come back. I felt sick to my stomach. I called to her—using the same tone of voice I had used in countless recall training drills. No Kaya. I called her again and again and silently prayed for help. And then—finally—I saw her running up the trail to me, limping badly and still crying and yelping. I fell to my knees to greet her, choking back the tears to remain calm to give her the energy she needed to feel safe. I told her what a good girl she was to come, over and over.

Besides the injury to her front leg, she had a gash on her ear that was bleeding. She was trembling and terrified. I was furious at myself for allowing this to happen to her. I had screwed up, big time, and my poor dog—who had been through so much and was just beginning to experience peace and happiness—had paid the price. I took her home and iced the leg, cleaned up her ear, massaged her, and fed her lots of yummy things. It was too late to take her to the vet, but I would bring her in Monday morning. I knew it could wait till Monday because, while she was limping on the leg, she was putting at least, some weight on it. The ear I could deal with myself.

When my vet examined Kaya's leg Monday, she said it was a bad sprain. These kinds of injuries might heal and be fine or could mean a weak leg for the rest of Kaya's life. She told me to rest it and just let Kaya go for minimal leashed outings to relieve herself for at least two weeks. We did as we were told, and then some. Kaya limped on and off for several months. Since the incident, even after allowing it time to heal, the leg has given Kaya trouble occasionally. But that is not the only scar that the attack left on Kaya. I now had a leash-reactive dog to deal with.

Leash reactivity is when a dog reacts to another dog by becoming highly agitated, barking, lunging, and pulling on the leash. This is a fear-induced behavior, where the dog is trying to fend off an attack before it happens. Kaya had not exhibited any of this behavior before the attack. But now, she was into it big time. My enjoyable, peaceful walks were now stressful and difficult any time she passed another dog. I began the arduous task of rehabilitation.

My dog, who was just learning to trust, had once again had her trust betrayed. And I should have known better. I vowed that I would never again let human social considerations cloud my judgment in choosing which dogs I would let my dog interact with. From now on I would only let Kaya greet calm, stable dogs. And even that could only happen when we had the leash reactivity under control. That could take an extended period of time and relentless, patient counter-conditioning.

The way this worked was, every day, I walked her with a container of tiny pieces of dog treats that I had made with a pill splitter. I kept her far enough away from other dogs that she didn't react, and told her she was a good girl and treated her every time we passed a dog that she didn't react to. As time went by, I gradually moved her closer and closer to other dogs, and started feeding her treats before she reacted, always praising and rewarding her when she didn't react. Eventually, if it worked, Kaya would look forward to dogs approaching because it meant treats. This is a very tricky maneuver, because if you misjudge and the other dog involved reacts, it is a huge setback, and can cost you months or even years.

Unfortunately, there are people who just refuse to listen when you tell them no. Every time one of them with a hyper, out-of-control dog barges over and sets off a reaction from the dog you are training, you have lost hard-earned progress you have made in this very tedious training. But I was determined to undo the harm I had allowed to be done. Ultimately, it took two and a half years to undo the damage from the attack. But I am so proud of Kaya. I can now walk her past an out-of-control, barking, lunging dog, and she totally ignores it. Sometimes she looks at me and makes eye contact, as if to tell me that she totally understands I don't want her to do that, and wants me to notice how good she's being. So I give her a reward. I always do because she has really earned it.

Training isn't something you do for a while and then it's done, any more than a diet is done when you lose weight. If you don't continue to eat differently, you will gain all the weight back. I know this because

I have done it seventy-nine times! If you want to have a calm, balanced, polite dog, you must work with him or her on an ongoing basis. I happen to enjoy working with dogs immensely, because it is much more likely to be effective than trying to rehabilitate humans! Training should be fun and enjoyable for both the dog and the human. I have never had a dog who didn't love to work and learn. Kaya was no exception, and she was a quick study for obedience work. The leash reactivity, however, was a real challenge. It would have been so much easier to have prevented it in the first place. Lesson learned: Be very, very, particular which dogs you let you dog interact with.

She just calmly slept there---
exactly as Lakota would have done.

CHAPTER THIRTY-FOUR:

Musical Mystery Tour: October 2017

It has been almost ten months since I have wanted to pick up my guitar and play and sing. Since doing this has been a lifelong joy of mine, this is one of the longest periods of time I have ever gone without doing it. I have avoided it because I have known what would happen if I did it: Because it connects so directly with my emotions, it would open the well, break the dam, and unplug the stopper of my loss.

There are people who can sing while they are crying. I have seen them on reality singing shows. I have also seen people who can talk while they are crying. I have seen them on the news. There are also people who can look good while they are crying. I have seen them on celebrity awards shows. I am not like any of these people. When I cry I do not have that kind of control. I knew from past experience that the minute I started to sing, all my feelings about the loss of Lakota would open up, if I had not healed sufficiently from my loss. It would be full frontal, gut-wrenching, contact-lens-blurring sobbing, floods of tears, snot running down my face onto my guitar. It would be a typhoon; and it would not be pretty. I would be choking and I would not be able to sing a note. It is quite a bit of work to set up my equipment, and I didn't want to do it or ask Bill to do it and then not be able to proceed. And so, I had not picked up my guitar since before Lakota had been critically ill.

But on this particular night, I felt the old craving. Kaya had never been exposed to my musical sideline, and because I played an electric-acoustic guitar, it had to be plugged into an amp, and I used a mike. The volume could only go down so low. Because of her anxiety issues, and because a lot of dogs are noise sensitive and/or noise fearful, I was worried that she might be frightened by this new sound. I also wondered how she would deal with all the wire, and if she would be a problem pulling them out or knocking things over.

This had happened with Lakota when he was a puppy, and we had to remove him and gate him in the kitchen where he could watch from a distance without creating chaos or electrocuting one of us. He was so upset that he couldn't be next to his mommy that every time I went to play after that, he completely avoided all the wires. When I played, he walked in a big circle around me and lay behind me and to the left, by the wall. If he accidently walked where he got tangled in a wire, he would freeze in place and not move until someone came and carefully removed the wire. This behavior became a useful skill when he became a therapy dog: Lakota could visit people with I.V.s, tubes, wires from electrical devices, and so on, and be trusted to not pull them out. He was often called upon to visit fragile patients because he was so trustworthy. It had always fascinated me how two seemingly unrelated activities had been linked together, with one preparing Lakota to do his job even better, when working at the other.

Kaya was an active dog with anxiety, and big enough to do damage to my equipment, so the question of how she would react was foremost in my mind after we set up and I got ready to sit down and tune up. Kaya was my Velcro dog. She came into the bathroom with me, followed me everywhere I went, and off-leashed with a recall that took my breath away. She was not fond of being separated from me at all. So imagine my surprise when I strapped on my guitar, wove my way through the wires, and sat down, and—instead of bulling her way through to get close to me—she calmly walked around the setup, tracing the same path that Lakota used to take, and went to lie down in the very same spot, under the dining room table, that he used to occupy when I practiced. Furthermore, she didn't bat an eye or flick an ear when I started to play. She just calmly slept there—exactly as Lakota would have done. And she stayed there for two hours and didn't move—exactly as Lakota would have done. And then, when I got up, she carefully wound her way around the setup to me in the living room and got all excited because she knew she had been a good girl and would get cheese—exactly as Lakota would have done. Did he tutor her? I mean, what are the odds that this high-anxiety dog with OCD chewing issues would have acted this way on her own, when exposed to this for the first time?

I called Kaya out of her den,
brought her into the bedroom,
and got her up on the bed
so I could see better.

CHAPTER THIRTY-FIVE:

Dog Vet Double Header: May 29, 2018

As I mentioned earlier, several vets over the years have told me how often, when they put a dog on a medication for a particular condition, it turns out that the owner is on the same medication for a similar condition. I don't know why this is. Perhaps there are environmental factors affecting both the dog and the human. However, this theory falls apart when there are other family members in the same environment, with similar genetic backgrounds, who do not have the same issues.

My approach to our animals has become more spiritual since 11/13/11—the day The Zeakie Dog crossed over the Rainbow Bridge. I believe our dogs and other animals come to us for spiritual reasons. It is my opinion that some are sent to love and support us because we need that. I think that some come to us to teach us lessons we want or need to learn. And, in the case of those with similar medical issues to their humans, I believe some come and to share or take over some of our physical/medical burdens to help us.

I have been a person with a lot of allergies, asthma, and digestive problems for my whole life. So it is not surprising to me that Kaya has similar issues. She has serious food allergies, seasonal allergies, skin itching issues, skin rash issues, digestive issues, and a collapsing trachea. I have gone to great lengths to help my girl with these issues. It has not been easy. Not only does she have these problems, but the medications that would help these problems cause her other serious digestive problems, so she can't take most of them. This leaves me battling the problems with the few meds she can tolerate, and the rest have to be managed with "lifestyle changes." Coincidently, or perhaps not, I am in the exact same situation with my own medical issues and the medications to manage them.

We currently have Kaya's food allergies addressed. We visited a veterinary nutritionist at the top animal facility in the state, and with her help, Kaya is doing well and not experiencing any food-related issues at this writing. I know this because she has gone through the whole winter without any digestive or itching problems. It has been a beautiful, peaceful time when we can actually go somewhere in the car with her without Bill or I having to watch in a mirror to see if she is licking herself to the point of injury in the back seat.

But this tranquility ends for her—as it does for me—in February. Towards the end of February tree pollen starts to appear, and the misery starts for both of us. Itchy runny eyes, sneezing, runny nose, and migraines for me—and, for Kaya, the skin itching begins. It starts off slowly with just some occasional scratching and escalates as we go through spring.

Not only do I have a very itchy dog, but when she is stressed, as she is by itching, she also exhibits obsessive/compulsive behavior and ELS, an acronym for excessive licking syndrome. So when she has an itch and starts licking it, she doesn't stop. This can and does produce some nasty rashes, wounds, and abrasions. I am not a fan of sticking an e-collar (cone) on a dog's head without first relieving the itch. Imagine how you would feel if someone did that to you. Intense itching can be as bad as pain. To further complicate the situation, Kaya has a double coat so thick that it is impossible to see her skin. Finding a tick in her fur is incredibly difficult until the tick is attached and engorged and it may be too late by then to prevent transfer of disease, so I am very diligent about tick control. It is also very difficult to tell if she has a rash where her fur is thickest until it gets bad enough to show through the fur. When you add in all of these factors, as you can well imagine, we are at the vet a lot.

On this particular day, in late May of 2018, I was brushing Kaya's teeth and grinding her nails with a Dremel tool when I discovered a nasty-looking wound in the area where her back leg attached to her abdomen. This happens to be an area rich in itch receptors and is a common site for itching problems. She must have done a real number on it while we were sleeping, and it looked bad enough that I didn't want to try to treat it myself without getting serious itch relief from the vet, so Kaya wasn't tormented with itching while also being miserable in a cone. I was also concerned about infection, so off to the vet we went.

When we had called in for the appointment I had been told that our vet was away and that there was a covering vet there, so I was not surprised to see an unfamiliar face when we went into the examining room. We got an unhappy but cooperative Kaya onto the examining table, and the vet looked at her flank and prescribed steroid/antibiotic spray. Steroid/antibiotic spray fixes just about anything that goes wrong on a dog's skin, with a few exceptions, such as fungal infections. So we paid the bill and left and I thought that would be the end of it.

We went home and had lunch, I took Kaya for a late walk, and then went into the office to work. The gift we had recieved had paid off our mortgage, allowing us to put a small addition on our home and now we had an office on the main floor.

Kaya had a den under my worktable where she took naps while I worked. But my concentration was broken by hearing an unfamiliar sound coming from Kaya's den. It sounded like she was chewing and sucking like she used to do to blankets when we first got her. When I knelt down to see what she was doing, I could see that she wasn't gnawing on a blanket this time... she was gnawing on herself!

I called her out of her den, brought her into the bedroom, and got her up on the bed so I could see better. I got the small but powerful LED light I use for such things and shone it on the area of her attention: it was over her right hip to the right of her tail. I couldn't see a thing wrong...until I started digging deeply into her thick undercoat. When I got down far enough, white stuff started coming to the surface. The more I disturbed the area, the more white stuff came up. It was a mess, but her fur was so thick that I couldn't really see her skin, no matter what I did. But when I rubbed a tissue on the area after parting her fur, some blood was on it. I had never seen anything quite like this, so back to the vet.

We got Kaya back up on the dreaded table and the vet started trying to part the dense coat to see what was going on. She commented that this was one of the densest coats she had seen in her many years as a vet. This surprised me because when I adopted Kaya she appeared to be a short-haired dog. Evidently, that was not true, especially when it came to her back end. There, she had a dense undercoat—the kind I had always heard referred to as a double coat. The vet told me Kaya would have to be shaved to see what the problem was and to treat it. Then she got a clipper and set to the task. Mounds of fluff began piling up—more and more. The clippers labored valiantly to keep up with volume, but finally gave up and clogged. The vet handed the clippers to her tech, who started working to unclog them. Meanwhile, the vet started working on the fur with a shedding comb. There were no mats and no knots and nothing to tip me off that there was a problem under Kaya's fur—one had to dig deeply to find it. From the surface it didn't even look like she had a thick coat, and the brush I used on her always just glided through her fur, but this dog was a fur factory, and the vet was describing it as a triple coat. Somewhere in Kaya's family history there must be some northern breed to have a coat like this. I had never had a dog with such a coat, and from now on, I was going to have to be much more proactive about stripping the undercoat out.

The tech came in with the now revived clippers and more shaving ensued. We could have filled the better part of a grocery bag with fur. Then the clipper protested again. More clipper rehab—more shaving, and on and on until the clipper died right as we finally reached the Holy Grail: Kaya's skin. It was a mess. The vet described it as seborrhea dermatitis. It had probably started as just an itch that Kaya got into licking till the undercoat was so saturated it couldn't dry. She prescribed a prescription medicated shampoo to be followed by a prescription medicated mousse. She said that this would be a problem every spring unless I did serious, deep shedding with her starting in February. And even then, it was possible she might have to be shaved preemptively if I couldn't get enough fur out to let her skin breathe.

Since poor Kaya had spent much of the day at her least favorite place, I decided to stop at the park on the way home and give her a little outing. I wasn't prepared for the embarrassment factor that would be a part of our walks for the next few weeks:

"O.M.G, look at that dog's butt!"

"What happened? Did she sit in something?"

"Eeeeuuwww…is that contagious?"

"Look, Mommy, that dog has a butt like those baboons we saw at the zoo!"

The variations on people's reactions to Kaya's shaved rear end went on for about three weeks. By then the creeping crud had been eliminated and enough fur had grown in to hide the fact that she had been shaved. While I found it rather embarrassing, Kaya seemed unperturbed by the butt shaming. Mercifully, no wise guys took pictures and posted them on social media, sparing us that humiliation. I vowed that the following February I would make thorough grooming and thinning of Kaya's undercoat a daily event in hopes of avoiding this.

Whether I would be successful remained to be seen, because the time of year when she began to shed was the same time of year she got itchy from seasonal allergies, and that triggered her excessive licking syndrome. So far, her digestive system had protested the use of any and all prescriptions designed to stop the itching. I have tried numerous holistic products to no avail. I will continue searching for a solution. I have made peace with the fact that the Lord has sent me "Miss High Maintenance" to care for because I am in a position to do that. Someone working would have a breakdown trying to keep up with these issues. She is definitely worth it and deserves a break because most or all of these issues were probably caused by neglect: poor management of her and the other puppies in her litter, including how much time they had with their mother and siblings, poor nutrition, crowding, and terrible stress.

It was her belief that God entrusted these special animals
to our care because he knew we would give them
the love and extra care they needed,
and blessed us with the resources to do so.

CHAPTER THIRTY-SIX:

Why I Can't Sleep at Night Part I: June 2018

Having spent one month short of two years with Kaya, I had become suspicious that something was wrong with one of her hips. I wanted to know what was up with it so we didn't do anything to make it worse and to be sure we were exercising her appropriately. So I discussed it with our vet and we decided to take X-rays. As long as she was under sedation, I asked that her bloodwork that was due be done to save her that unpleasantness.

The X-rays revealed that, on one side, Kaya had no hip joint at all. It was so malformed that there was no bone connection. The joint was being held together by soft tissues. Thankfully, the other side was good. This explained why Kaya ran at a kind of skewed angle. She was really fast, too, so while I expected an issue, I never expected she had such a major hip problem. However, I also didn't expect what her bloodwork turned up: Kaya had a slightly low cortisol level.

This was a concern, and my vet suggested testing for Addison's disease. Addison's disease is marked by an abnormally low level of cortisol, which is serious and can even be fatal. President John F. Kennedy had it, and historians have written a lot about how the fact that he had to take Prednisone may have altered some of his decisions. That is because Prednisone can alter mood and cause irritability. Addison's can be very dangerous, because if it is undetected, the first time it presents itself can be a full-blown Addisonian crisis which is often fatal. Furthermore, stress is a major factor in Addison's, and Kaya had been through a lot before we got her. Her anxiety, OCD, and collapsing trachea didn't come out of nowhere. This presented a difficult situation because going to the vet is a major stressor. The test required fasting and two blood draws, a couple of hours apart. After the first blood draw, a stimulating injection would be given. The second blood draw would measure the cortisol level reaction to the stimulating injection.

We wanted this to be as low-stress as possible, so we agreed that I would not leave Kaya at the vet the whole time. Of course, just fasting Kaya was a major ordeal. She had such anxiety about food—probably due to a period of starvation when she was abandoned and on her own—that not feeding her breakfast made me feel like some kind of monster. The look in her eyes just killed me. The plan was to take her to the vet as soon as the hospital opened. After the first blood draw and injection, I would take her to a nearby park and we would take a long, peaceful walk, and get back right on time for the second blood draw. The plan went well, we got everything done, Kaya got her breakfast, and now we had to wait for the results.

I was very uptight about the outcome, because if Kaya had Addison's she would have to be on Prednisone for the rest of her life. I didn't know how I could manage Kaya on Prednisone. Kaya could barely control herself around food. She was always ravenous and was obsessed with eating. Prednisone causes dogs to have insatiable appetites. My friend Donna had a dog on Prednisone and had a story to tell about this effect.

She had gone out to run a few errands, leaving a can of baked beans on the kitchen counter. She did not see this as a problem since the can was unopened. She came back an hour later to a shocking situation. Her dog, ravenous from the medication, had gotten up on the counter, taken the unopened can of beans, chewed open the metal can, and eaten the contents. The poor dog was a mess. His mouth was all cut up and blood was everywhere.

Kaya was *already* ravenous. I was afraid she would chew through the kitchen cabinets to get food if she had to go on Prednisone. So it was with great concern that I waited for the test results. A few days later my vet called. I got the call in my car on my Bluetooth, and was nearby, so I asked if I could stop by. She agreed and I was there in ten minutes. She took me to the computer and we viewed the lab report. Kaya had a slightly low cortisol level, but it was not at the level where it was considered Addison's. Dr. Rao also had consulted with Internal Medicine, and they agreed that it was not Addison's until it crossed that limit. That being said, we had to watch Kaya very carefully. This was such a close call that Dr. Rao told me we could put her on a low dose of Prednisone if I would feel safer. But Prednisone had other serious side effects besides the food issue. We agreed to not put Kaya on the drug, but to watch her carefully for any signs of Addison's.

I am not a fan of this type of situation. I have anxiety to begin with. I had been through a lot of dog trauma in the past few years. Now, once again, I had a potentially life-threatening situation that could pop up suddenly, and if I didn't happen to be near the vet's at the time it could be a disaster. However, the worst thing—the thing that could push this over the edge—was stress. Kaya needs to lead a low-stress life. Since she picks up my every emotion, that means I have to be a beacon of calmness while dealing with this worrisome situation.

This is kind of like my situation with sleeping. I have been an insomniac since nineteen sixty-eight. That's when my son was born. My husband was in Vietnam and I had moved in with my parents while he was overseas. After I gave birth, I didn't want the baby to wake my parents, so I was in a state of hyper-vigilance all night, so I could get up and comfort him at the first peep he made. Decades later, I still can't turn that hyper-vigilant state off. It came in handy when Zeak and Lakota were sick and I had to monitor them. But it was a rare thing for me to get a full night's sleep. Numerous doctors' appointments had never helped the problem. I have tried over-the-counter medications, prescription medications, meditation, deep breathing, Yoga breathing, 4-7-8 breathing, relaxation techniques, military sleep techniques, white noise, pink noise, music, special lighting, darkness, getting out of bed, staying in bed, watching TV, not watching any devices for three hours before bed, reading, and practicing what they call, "good sleep hygiene." None of it has worked.

But staying up all night is not the worst part of it. The worst part of it is hearing how not getting a full night's sleep can cause heart attacks, strokes, Alzheimer's Disease, Dementia, cancer, and a host of other illnesses! So I lie there and stress about the fact that I can't sleep, which contributes to my not being able to fall asleep. Now I can also stress about my dog. Is the sweet, beautiful Kaya, sleeping so peacefully next to me (no insomnia for her!) a walking time bomb? At times like this I remind myself to think positively and have faith. Of course, the more times you do that and then get clobbered, the more difficult it becomes to sustain that faith. But I always seem to find a way to go back to my spiritual well, take a drink, and come up with some more faith. But that doesn't happen until dawn. That's when I get up.

Elaine and I had discussed our "high-maintenance" dogs before. We took better care of our dogs than anyone we knew, so why all these medical problems? Elaine always had some wise, spiritual perspective on things. It was one of her gifts. It was her belief that God entrusted these special animals to our care because he knew we would give them the love and extra care they needed, and blessed us with the resources to do so. That felt so much better than thinking my beautiful dogs were being picked on! So I chose to adopt Elaine's uplifting perspective and be grateful for the gift of such a wonderful friend. Now, if only she could help me sleep...

The dragon-snake is what I called cancer after
a dream I had when Zeakie was fighting for his life.
In the dream I was fighting this cancer beast
in the form of a dragon-snake out on the lake.
It had first taken Zeak, and then, Lakota.

CHAPTER THIRTY-SEVEN:

Why I Can't Sleep at Night Part II: October 2018

I brush my dogs' teeth every day. I do it to save them the pain of dental problems. It also saves me the large expense of cleanings, because the way I do it is so effective that none of my dogs has ever needed a professional tooth cleaning, and I have their teeth checked by the vet regularly. The reason they have never needed their teeth professionally cleaned is that I brush their teeth with such an effective tool that it keeps their teeth spotless. When I told my former vet about this, his tech said if she did that to her dog she would have to scrape him off the ceiling. What is this device that the tech thought would cause such a reaction in her dog? It was a simple, battery-operated, electric toothbrush for humans.

I found it very concerning that somebody who couldn't calmly condition her dog to accept an electric toothbrush was working as a vet tech. That was just one of the many reasons I left that practice. But I digress. Anyway, on this particular morning, as I did every morning, I cut up a bunch of dog treats with a pill splitter, so Kaya could get lots of them and not gain weight, and invited her into the bedroom to have her teeth brushed and her nails done.

The treats were the reason she calmly submitted to these tasks. The nails were not fun because they were painful. Kaya had been so neglected when she was picked up by rescue that her nails were very, very long…so long that it was difficult for her to walk. Inside of a dog's outer nail is a soft cuticle that is full of blood vessels and nerves called the quick. When you cut a dog's nails, if you cut into the quicks, two things happen, and both are unpleasant. The first thing will happen is that they bleed, and you will need styptic powder to stop the bleeding. The second thing that occurs is pain—pain similar to a dentist drilling into a nerve without anesthesia. All of this was further complicated by the fact that Kaya's nails were jet black so you couldn't see where the quicks were, and her nails grew incredibly fast. Due to long term neglect, the quicks in Kaya's nails would not recede to the point that the nails could be cut to a healthy length.

I had to devise a way to deal with this, and the only way I could come up with was to grind her nails with a Dremel tool every single day for just a second. She calmly lay on her side when I did this because she got a treat for each paw I did. I think she must have somehow remembered how much worse it could be if I didn't do that, and that also encouraged her to cooperate. Her nails would never be the proper length, but my vet said that this kept them at a length where they weren't doing damage. If we didn't do this and keep them under control, it could cause painful infections at the base of the nail (the equivalent of a human ingrown toenail) and shoulder problems.

Finished with her nails, I set to the task of brushing Kaya's teeth. I put the toothpaste on the brush and gently put my hand on top of her muzzle to open her mouth. I started to put the toothbrush between her lip and her teeth, when all of a sudden, a marble-sized ball of flesh flipped out of her mouth. It was attached to her lip and was mostly black like the rest of her gums and lips. The sight of it struck terror in my heart because I knew that anything growing in a dog's mouth is not good. I quickly finished brushing her teeth and then called my vet.

Dr. Rao was as concerned as I was, and I was grateful when she told me to come right in. She took one look at the growth and declared that it had to come out and right away. She told me to fast Kaya for surgery first thing the next morning.

The surgery went well and the growth was sent out for biopsy. It took about five days to get the biopsy report back. When I got the call I went right in to discuss the results with the vet and to have Kaya's surgery site checked.

Dr. Rao was trying to sound conversational because I'm sure she knew what the word that was about to come out of her mouth was going to do to my gut. "The growth on Kaya's lip was a melanoma, she said calmly." I kept my composure as she told me more, but my insides were screaming. The report said that it had all been removed and that the margins were clean but narrow. She then said that if it was her dog, she would do nothing more than watch it from here, but if I wanted to, I could certainly consult oncology.

I drove home trying to process this latest occurrence. First my four-year-old Zeakie came down with a deadly cancer and, with his oncologist Dr. Seiford, waged a fierce battle with it until he lost the fight at age five. He did not depart without blessing me with a profound, spiritual goodbye gift that rocked my world, changed me forever, and opened me up to being able to detect his continuing presence. All of these remarkable events are chronicled in *Walking with the Shadow of Love*. But nonetheless, I lost my magnificent, cherished dog at only five years of age, despite giving him the best care that was humanly possible.

Then, as detailed in this book, I lost Lakota to cancer: This time it was probably Leukemia and lung or sinus cancer, and at the end it was probably all through his body. In the period of five years I had my heart ripped out twice. I wound up with gastritis and an ulcer from it all. And now, only two years later, and this beast of a disease is going after Kaya?

Statistics tell us one out of three dogs under the age of ten and one out of every two dogs over the age of ten will get cancer. But we were running three out of three, and two of them were young dogs. I wondered aloud if the dragon-snake had some kind of vendetta against me and my dogs. The dragon-snake is what I called cancer after a dream I had when Zeakie was fighting for his life. In the dream I was fighting this cancer beast in the form of a dragon-snake out on the lake, smashing it with my paddle every time it surfaced. I thought I was done with it. I couldn't believe it was here again.

As I felt the fear rising in me, I had to remind myself of what we all need to remember at times like this: No one is ever taken from us. We perceive it as our loved ones being taken because their physical bodies are taken. But their soul—the essence of who they are—is immortal and indestructible, and is always with us. I have been told by my spiritual mentor that our animals can actually do more to help us when they are in spirit form. They will continue to love us, listen to us, and guide us until we are united with them. It is painful after they leave because we miss those hugs and kisses and that physical presence. But we must remember that they are not gone…they are still with us, just in a different form.

Poor Kaya had such an awful, traumatic life before I adopted her. I wanted her to have the best rest-of-her-life with me. I wanted to fill it with good food, beautiful long walks in the woods together, mental stimulation befitting her great intelligence and work ethic, and peaceful, soft, comfortable surroundings, so she felt safe and loved…for a change. And now we are being hit with this?

As I filled Elaine in on the latest events, she asked me if I was going to consult oncology. She felt that it would be better if I knew I had done everything possible for Kaya in case things didn't go well. I explained to her that I was concerned about the stress that all of these vet visits would cause Kaya and the effect on the Addison's Disease issue. I was truly torn because I had a lot of faith in my vet's instincts. For a week I went back and forth trying to make a decision. I finally decided that I needed to get a second opinion from Dr. Seiford, the oncologist who did such an incredible job giving Zeakie fifteen good months, against all odds, when he was struck with a disease so deadly it could have taken him out in a few days.

So I picked up the phone and called the facility where she worked, Animals First. I asked to speak to Catherine, Dr. Seiford's technician in oncology who had been so kind with Zeak. She came right to the phone. I told her what was going on, and she told me that Dr. Seiford was out on leave and would not be back for months. My heart dropped a beat. Catherine went on to say that they had a covering oncologist—a Dr. Jacobs—who could help us evaluate Kaya's biopsy report, and give a second opinion on the best course of action.

I explained to Catherine that my new rescue was a complicated case. I told her that Kaya was a rescue that had suffered some kind of hardship or trauma and had anxiety disorder and OCD. The case was further complicated by the fact that she had a low cortisol level—one approaching Addison's disease—and that stress was the major factor in Addison's. For that reason, I was concerned about the stress of veterinary care. I asked Catherine to level with me about how understanding the substitute vet would be about this issue. Catherine assured me that he was very kind. I told her that I would like to bring Kaya in just to have a second opinion on the report and a quick look at her lip so we could discuss outlook and options. I wanted to be sure all the bases were covered.

At the appointed day and time I drove with Kaya to Animals First. Catherine and I exchanged warm hugs. "I'm happy to see you, but I'm sorry you're here. O.M.G., Kaya looks like a smaller version of Zeak!" she exclaimed. She then went on to tell me she had rescued a dog who looked much like Kaya and also had anxiety disorder and OCD.

An unmistakable bond had formed between Catherine, Dr. Seiford, and I as we waged a full-out war against the cancer that sought to end the life of The Zeakie Dog. We had worked as a team, hitting the dragon-snake from every angle we could, and before we lost the war, we won many battles. And while we may have been defeated in the long run, we gave Zeakie, who was only five years old, a beautiful, joyful, fifteen-month life extension during which he ran and played, enjoyed his favorite foods, and felt well, and even enthusiastically did his job bringing joy into the days of many seniors in facilities. And when all was said and done, the dragon-snake knew it had been in a hell of a fight.

Five years later, Lakota had been taken by the same beast. And now, I was here with Kaya—who had been through more misery than any dog should have to endure—because it was now after her. A third of dogs under ten years old, and half of dogs over ten would get cancer. I repeated the statistics in my mind and wondered. I am so careful with my dogs. I feed them human-grade food or cook for them, guided by a veterinary nutritionist. I use only organics on my lawn. I clean with vinegar and baking soda whenever possible and remove the dogs from the area if I use anything else. We have a smoke-free home. We use stainless steel food and water bowls and water bottles. We vaccinate carefully. We do not frequent dog parks or board our dog or expose her to dogs we don't know are well cared for. What else does it take to keep your dog safe?

Many years ago I met a woman who was a medium. There was no internet then and she was states away from my home and did not know me. She was for real. She knew things about members of my family who had passed that no one could have known. Even my friends didn't know these things. One of the things she told me was that in the first three seconds we meet someone, our souls read each other, and we know what kind of person we have greeted. She said that if people would pay close attention to the *feeling* they get the first instant they meet someone, it would save a lot of heartache and misery. But we often override those feelings, talk ourselves out of them, or allow others to talk us out of them. Catherine led us into an exam room. Dr. Jacobs came in through another entrance and I instantly felt good about him.

He reviewed the biopsy report, looked in Kaya's mouth, and educated me about canine melanomas. I had no idea that there were two different kind of melanomas that this could be. If it were a skin melanoma that would be great news, because there was a ninety percent chance that it would not recur. The report said that Dr. Rao had successfully removed all of the growth, but that the margins were narrow. It was in a difficult spot: Remove too much and Kaya's mouth would not function properly anymore.

He then told me that the other possibility was that it was a mouth melanoma. If it were, it could be deadly, and it would probably already have metastasized. A likely place would be the lung. He suggested we do X-rays of Kaya's lungs, and we send the X-rays to him to review, if we decided to take them. He said that this type of cancer did not respond well to chemotherapy. Surgery, radiation, and a new immune vaccine were the only options, and even then, the prognosis was not good. We could give the vaccine now as a preemptive treatment if we wanted to.

I thanked him and Catherine, and took Kaya home. I had a lot to think about. Much of it would occur during the time that the rest of the world was sleeping.

Meanwhile, I did my best to stay in the present,
and Kaya and I enjoyed daily walks
in the snowy woods with Elaine and Cooper.

CHAPTER THIRTY-EIGHT:

The Christmas Gift: October-December 2018

I spent the next month thinking about, doing research about, and meditating and asking guidance for, what to do about Kaya. I prayed to Jesus, my angels and guides, and St. Francis, and asked Lakota and Zeak to show me the way. It was the spiritual equivalent of a police All Points Bulletin. At times I asked myself how I could still do this, after losing Zeak and Lakota despite so many prayers. While losing him was just as painful, at least Lakota lived a slightly longer than average life for a Labrador. But losing a dog as special as Zeak when he was so young seemed so unfair. But fair is not what this place called the physical world is about, and I have been blessed with too many contacts from the spiritual world to lose my faith.

A friend of mine had been battling Leukemia and had recently had immune therapy. It made him very sick. It added to his suffering and did not save him. There may be a cure someday, but we're not there yet. When I looked into the vaccine, I found that despite it being widely recommended by veterinary oncologists, studies had not borne out that it was significantly effective other than buying the dog some months. I would definitely do it if it gave Kaya extra months. However, Kaya had gotten sick from almost every medicine she had ever taken. Thankfully, she could tolerate antibiotics, but other meds that most dogs had no problem with, she vomited from, had diarrhea from, or both. Like her owner, she was extremely sensitive to medication. That made the likelihood very high that the immune vaccine would make her ill. I would not do anything that would cause a dog with such anxiety to suffer. So I crossed the vaccine off my list of choices.

Next I considered having X-rays done. Kaya had been sedated at Dr. Rao's before with no ill effects. Dr. Rao let me stay with her while they put her under, and had me there with her when they reversed the sedation so she woke up with me talking to her, thus minimizing her fear. I felt it was worth it to know if the melanoma had spread. It was mid-November when we took the X-rays and sent them to Animals First for Dr. Jacobs to review. Dr. Rao said she would let me know as soon as she heard from him.

A week passed and I didn't hear from Dr. Rao, so I called her. She told me she had called twice about the X-rays, but her calls had not been returned. Thanksgiving came and went, and still there was no word. Meanwhile, I did my best to stay in the present, and Kaya and I enjoyed daily walks in the snowy woods with Elaine and Cooper.

Every year since Zeak had passed, the first week of December, I have taken a cookie platter to Animals First, and some other kind of treat for the Oncology Department, to wish everyone happy holidays and remember them for all they did for my dogs. Many of the vets there had waived their fees to help us with the expensive treatments. Some of them cited Zeak's service as a therapy dog—some just did it to help with the bills. The vast majority of the huge expenses were the pharmaceuticals, not the vets or the facility. And so, the first week of December, I picked up the platter and headed to Animals First with Kaya. I had no intention of doing anything other than dropping off the gifts. But that was not the way it played out when I got there.

I dropped off the gifts and was about to leave when Catherine came out and saw me. She said, *"I can't believe you are here!"* I asked her why and she told me that Dr. Jacobs had just picked up Kaya's x-rays to look at them right before I walked in. She said that they had just seen their last patient, and here I was at the exact time when they were looking at Kaya's X-rays, and the perfect time to get the results. She said they had been booked so heavily the last few weeks with Dr. Seiford out that they were way behind, and for me to be here at the precise minute that they finally got to review Kaya's results was extraordinary.

I told her that had not been my intention when I came—I was just playing Santa—but I believed that someone was helping me to get here at this precise point in time—this seemed to be a lovely validation that there was a hand guiding all of this. I mean, what are the odds of this happening? Anytime I ask myself that question, I know there is help from the spirit world going on.

Catherine said that we could go into an exam room and find out what Dr. Jacobs saw in the X-rays immediately, so Kaya and I followed her into the same room we were in last time. As we walked in, a picture of Zeak on the wall of the room caught my eye and I got a chill and a strong sense that this was his work.

Dr. Jacobs entered from the other door with a smile on his face. He told us that as far as he could see from the X-rays, there was no sign of any disease. I felt warm tears fill my eyes. First the incredible timing of our arrival and now this wonderful news…it was overwhelming. The odds were now in our favor. From what I had read, if this were the deadly mouth melanoma, it would be all over the place by now. Dr. Jacobs said to keep a close check on her mouth. I assured him I would. I thanked him for seeing us without an appointment, gave Catherine a hug, and went to the front desk to pay the bill. When I asked about the bill, the receptionist said there was no charge.

Merry Christmas to us! I don't think my feet ever touched the ground as I walked to the SUV with Kaya.

Every week I do a meditation with each of my departed dogs. After I have achieved a calm, relaxed meditative state and quieted my mind—no easy task for me—I call out my dog's name three times and ask them if there is anything they want me to know. I picture them in front of me and feel us connected at the heart. I almost always get an immediate image in my mind. After years of doing this, I get recurring images for each of my dogs. I get stars from Zeak and hearts from Lakota. I frequently find stars and hearts in unexpected places now. They can't all be random events. An example of this was the time I randomly chose a path to walk across a huge field, and right in front of me—I would have stepped on it if I didn't stop—was a pretty, blue, glitter heart.

As I drove down the road to the park,
I looked up and there was a star formation
in the clouds.

CHAPTER THIRTY-NINE:

Animal Endangerment: May 2019

I am not a brave person. In fact, I am a nervous wreck! I suffer from anxiety for reasons stemming from both genetics and childhood experiences. For that reason, I am in awe of the brave: First responders are my heroes, our troops have my undying respect, and rescue teams, nurses, and doctors are held in my highest esteem. I have always wondered what I would do if I were put in a situation with even the tiniest amount of danger, because just being in an elevator causes me to have a panic attack that could trigger a cardiac event or a stroke. My super-sensitive empath body cannot deal with stress, and I have other serious health issues that dictate I must stay calm and relaxed, or I am in trouble.

But on this particularly beautiful spring day in May of 2019, as I was walking Kaya out to my vehicle to go to the park, I saw something that caused me to spring into action like some kind of action hero. This was no big deal like running into a burning building to save someone. It was pretty low risk, but for me, any risk is too scary, so I have no idea how I was able to do any of this. I just know it didn't come from me—it came *through* me, and I definitely had some kind of help.

Kaya and I had just reached the side of the road when a car came down the road at a pretty good clip WITH A DOG TIED TO THE CAR DOOR, RUNNING ALONGSIDE, DESPERATELY TRYING TO KEEP UP WITH THE VEHICLE! When the dog saw Kaya, it reacted, which caused it to lose its forward rhythm. The driver of the car looked at the dog, and yelled "Hey!" out the window, but kept moving, approaching a crossroad intersection in that distracted state. The dog could have been under the tires of the car in a split second if it made the slightest wrong move. I noticed the dog was wearing boots, which had to increase the likelihood of it stumbling, in which case it would be dragged by the car! In addition, our roads are so narrow that there is barely room for two cars to squeeze through. If another car came from the other direction, the dog would be run over by one car or the other.

I had to do something! I called the police and told the dispatcher what was happening and the general area where the vehicle with the dog tethered to it was going. I asked her to please send an officer right away before this dog was killed, and told the dispatcher that I would follow the vehicle and update the location. I then proceeded to do that. I followed at a distance so the driver didn't get suspicious. The car drove to a parking lot down by our community beach and clubhouse. I parked unobtrusively and watched as the driver—a woman—got out, removed the dog's boots, and proceeded to get another dog out of the car and put boots on it and tie it to the car door. She was going to do the same thing to another dog! I called the police again and updated the location. I also took a photo of the car, the license plate, and the driver.

When I saw the direction she was headed, I went around the other way, intending to beat her to the road and delay her until the police got there. I got to the road before her, headed up it a short distance, and stopped right in the middle of the road, blocking her from being able to pass. I called the police and told them where we were. Then I had to think fast, because I was terrified of getting into a confrontation with her. I gestured a few times, shrugging my shoulders, and called out the window that I was stuck. She pulled into a driveway to turn around and go the other way. I prayed for help—I couldn't stop her if she turned around. By now I was shaking from anxiety. I couldn't let her get away. This woman was either sadistic, mentally ill, or, incredibly ignorant of how dangerous what she was doing was to these helpless animals. What would she do to Kaya and me now that we were obstructing her? And where were the police?

It was then that I got the help I prayed for, but it wasn't from the police—at least not yet—it was from a gas company! A very large truck that took up most of the narrow road came toward us from the other direction, blocking the woman with the car with the dogs in it. The woman was now putting the dog in the car. Perhaps she was getting suspicious. I ran over to the gas truck and asked the driver if he would please just wait a minute and stay put. He didn't even roll his window down and seemed disinterested. In a louder voice I said, "Please—I need help!" Then he rolled down his window. I told him what had transpired and that the police were on the way, but that I needed him to block the road until they arrived. He agreed to do that.

I went back to my SUV, locked the doors, and waited for another couple of minutes until the police finally arrived. I got out of my vehicle and ran over to the police car, my heart pounding. When I told him what the woman had been doing to the dogs, he said, "That's crazy!" I told him that I was actually very concerned that this woman was crazy, and was worried about a confrontation, so I was so relieved to see him on the scene. I wondered aloud if the woman was running a dog walking business and doing that to her client's dogs. Or did these poor dogs belong to her? I told him I was available if he needed a witness, and he took my license number. I asked him if I needed to stay and he said I didn't. I thanked the driver of the gas truck and told him he might have saved the life of some dogs—I had no idea how many were in her car.

I got back in my vehicle and headed for my original destination—the park—for my morning hike with Kaya. I couldn't stop shaking. I tried to slow down my breathing and just focus on driving. *As I drove down the road to the park, I looked up and there was a star formation in the clouds. Since Zeak always sent me stars in unexpected places, I took that to be a reassurance that all would be OK. I was so elated by the sighting that I pulled over and took a picture with my phone. I wondered what kind of wind could possibly blow in five different directions to make a cloud star.* By the time I got to the park I wasn't shaking any more, but my hands were tingling, which really scared me because it meant my blood pressure was dangerously high. I decided the hike would help me release the stress, so we did the usual route.

When I got back home, my blood pressure was way up. I talked to my son and he told me to take my anxiety medication, which should help. He and I were both concerned about this woman retaliating. If she was mentally unbalanced she might do something to me or Kaya. I vowed to never let my dog out in our yard unless I was with her.

I then called our dog walker. She wanted to see the picture to see if she knew who it was, but both the person and the car were unfamiliar to her. She was very upset to hear that anyone in our community would do a thing like that. She said she was actually having heart palpitations thinking about it.

The whole thing left me shaken and unsettled. And now I wondered what lay ahead. What did the policeman do? I hope he called Animal Control and had the dogs removed from her possession and taken to a safe place until the owners could pick them up. What if she wasn't a dog walker? What if they were hers? Why did she put boots on the dogs? It wasn't hot at all—in fact it was chilly, so it wasn't to avoid burning their pads on a hot road. Was she trying to hide damage to their pads? Or did she actually care about the dogs but had no idea how dangerous what she was doing was? Would I be called in to testify?

It was these questions that were now keeping me up at night.

There have been times when I was facing medical procedures—a major anxiety for me—and was very fearful. But Lakota and/or Zeak showed up in some way to give me support. Sometimes I asked them to help and sometimes they just made their presence known, somehow knowing I needed them. One example of this occurred when I was facing a scary dentist appointment for a problem tooth. I got to the dentist early and decided to run into a supermarket across the street for an item I needed. As I was walking down the aisle of the store, a young man approached me. He introduced himself as a tech who had worked briefly for my vet. As soon as he said that, I remembered him. He told me that he recognized me, remembered what a beautiful black Labrador I had, and decided to say hello. He couldn't have been more than in his early twenties. Most men his age would be focused on other things and not have bothered to initiate a conversation with someone they had only met once or twice, or specifically mentioned my dog. He even remembered Lakota's name. It was surprising he remembered. It was the timing that made it a synchronicity. To me it was Lakota letting me know of his presence.

*The years had been kind to Cooper---
kinder than anyone would have expected.*

CHAPTER FORTY:

Cooper the Mighty Bear Hunter: July 2019

From the time my neighbor's dog, Cooper, had come into our lives—which I recounted in *Walking with the Shadow of Love*—he was Lakota and Zeak's pack member, which made him a member of our family. As a pack/family, we walked together, played together, ate together, spent holidays together, and even grieved together. With Lakota, Zeak, and Shy having crossed over (passed on), Cooper was the last of the great pack we had—the only surviving member, and he was getting old.

Cooper was a character. He was the calmest, most easygoing dog imaginable. I've mentioned before how Labradors have been split into two types: the field dog and the bench dog. But Cooper was his own dog, and with Cooper the world was introduced to a third type of Labrador: the couch dog. He was a mellow guy, and he never met a nap that he didn't love.

On any given day, Cooper might describe his schedule like this:

8:00 Up and out to relieve myself.

8:30 Wait patiently (it takes forever!) for Mommy to make my breakfast.

8:35 Eat my breakfast.

8:40 Out to relieve myself.

8:45 Back inside and onto the couch for my morning nap.

10:30 Mommy wakes me up from a perfectly good sleep to make me take a walk, though I don't want to.

10:35 She makes me go anyway—some nonsense about needing to exercise—whatever…

10:42 We get in the car and go to the park. We walk to the ballfield. I see Kaya. I know it irritates her if I run around, so I run around. She mistakes me for a sheep and starts herding me. I sit down so she can't nip at my heels. Ha, Ha, Kaya.

10:52 We head for the trail. Mommy wants to walk all the way up and down the mountain with Kaya and Aunt Margo, but I don't see the point because it takes longer to get back to the car that way. So I plant my feet and refuse to move. Mommy insists, so I have to go, but at least I get a cookie.

11:30 We get back to the car. I'm hungry and tired. We go home and have lunch (thankfully) and I can finally get back to my nap on the couch, which was so rudely interrupted.

12:30 Sleep on couch.

1:30 Sleep on couch.

2:00 Mommy wants to work in the yard. She brings me out with her and tethers me to the house near her.

2:05 Sleep in the yard in the sun.

2:30 Sleep in the yard in the shade.

3:00 Roll in the grass/snow depending on the time of year.

3:30 Relieve myself in the yard and then sleep some more.

4:00 Mommy wakes me up AGAIN and makes me go for yet another walk.

5:00 Dinner—it's about time. A guy could starve around here waiting to be fed.

5:30 Out to relieve myself.

6:00 Sleep on couch till bedtime.

9:30 Out to relieve myself.

10:00 Bed—thankfully—I've had an exhausting day.

There were days that Cooper and Elaine did therapy dog visits. There were occasional play dates. When Lakota and Zeak were in the physical world and Cooper was young, these play dates were very active. But the rest of the day was mostly nap, and now that Cooper was a senior, the play dates were just visits with naps on my couch.

Cooper's mellow nature made him a very easy dog to handle. He could handle meeting any dog. Even difficult, reactive, insecure dogs were not a problem. Cooper's calm demeanor put them at ease. That was why I had asked Elaine and Allie to bring him over when we rescued Kaya. She was a nervous wreck, and I knew that Cooper would be a big help in calming her down.

Sometimes, Cooper's calm manner would very suddenly flip to his playful side. This was usually triggered by another dog that he wanted to play with. Sometimes it was Kaya, sometimes it was other dogs at the park. He would go from calm and relaxed to what I called "helicopter jumping"—he would just vault straight up into the air as if he were on springs, over and over, and then launch into a burst of fast running. At this point, his back end would overtake his front end because he had too much torque, and he would roll over on his back in submission to whatever dog he was playing with.

The years had been kind to Cooper—kinder than anyone would have expected. Elaine and Allie were first-time dog owners, and they had no idea that the puppy they purchased from a local breeder was gravely ill. Cooper was so ill that, after tests and trials of medications with a veterinary internist failed, the specialist told them to put Cooper down. Elaine and Allie were not about to give up on their boy, so they took Cooper to a veterinary nutritionist at the best animal hospital in the state. The nutritionist did what the internist could not do: She saved the dog's life. How she did it was remarkable. She put him on a diet of pork tenderloin and garbanzo beans. This pricey diet, combined with supplements and a medication, completely fixed Cooper's problem. If Elaine and Allie had not bought Cooper and kept him, the unscrupulous breeder would have probably put him down.

So for almost ten years, his dedicated owners cooked pork tenderloin for Cooper and bought huge cans of garbanzo beans at Costco to keep their boy alive and well. Cooper thrived on his pork and beans and had a life that most dogs would envy...a life that he would not have had at all, had he not fallen into exactly the right hands.

That he was a happy boy was reflected by one of his most endearing characteristics: his smile. Lakota had smiled a lot. Zeak had also smiled a lot. But Cooper not only smiled: He worked it! If he wanted a cookie, he came up to you and grinned. If you were making dinner and it smelled good, he grinned. Even though he could never have any because of his stomach issues, hope sprang eternal in Cooper's doggy tummy, and he smiled a super-white, toothy grin that would put a movie star's flashy smile at a photo shoot to shame. It never failed to make us laugh—it was so funny and so human-looking.

So we now have this portrait of a super-mellow, easygoing guy who can get along with even the most difficult dogs, makes a full-time occupation of napping, and accents every precious moment with a smile. Cooper had always been a good watchdog, barking to alert his owners if someone came near the house. And on more than one occasion, he had stopped his owners from going into the woods—literally refusing to move—and they had found out soon afterwards that there had been a bear in the woods. But even that behavior did not predict what happened one very hot July afternoon in 2019.

When Elaine tended her garden, she brought Cooper out with her and tethered him to a metal fastener which was screwed into solid wood on the side of their house. It had been there for nine years—the same number of years that Cooper had been on this earth, and he was only a little over a week from his tenth birthday. Elaine only tethered Cooper if she was right there with him, but on this day, even staying with him didn't keep her boy out of trouble. Cooper was a geriatric old fellow now. He had a problem with a disc in his neck, arthritis throughout his body, and wasn't moving too fast anymore. The summer heat was really a problem for him and he could only go for short walks.

On this particular afternoon, I had met Elaine and Cooper in front of their house and we had taken a short walk together. The heat and the bad air quality had made me feel ill—these things are rough on asthma—so I went home to lie down for a while. As I was lying on my bed with Kaya, I heard some yelling in the distance, but I couldn't make out who it was or what they were yelling. Ours is a lake community with a lot of children, so yelling is not something alarming. But I found out later what all the fuss was about, and it was quite surprising.

Elaine was working in her garden and Cooper was napping by her, tethered to the house in the shade, when he was awakened by his nose. His nose had picked up a scent he didn't like because he felt it posed a threat to his mommy. He let out a roar/bellow/bark that made the hair on Elaine's arms stand on end. When she looked up, it was to see what appeared to be a 500-pound bear coming towards them on the road. That was enough for Cooper. Our mellow, Clark-Kent-like hero sprang into action. While he declined to don tights and a cape, he took off at the bear with such a fury that he ripped the tether out of the wall, charging down the street, leash, tether, and all. The bear took one look and decided that he didn't want to tangle with this charging black dog. Down the road he ran with a barking, growling Cooper in hot pursuit, and Elaine running after her dog, terrified, screaming at him to come back. The bear ran into the woods at the end of the street right about where Cooper ran out of adrenaline. Elaine finally caught up with him, relieved he was in one piece and hadn't suffered the same fate as Shy had when she had gone after a bear on a really hot day.

She took him home, brought him into the air conditioning, cooled him down, and said a prayer of thanks that she still had her boy to love. An unlikely superhero, Cooper grinned her into giving him a cookie, obviously proud of his accomplishment. Then…you guessed it…he took a long, long, nap.

The last of the great pack was about to depart from the physical world.

CHAPTER FORTY-ONE:

A Sudden Departure: August 2, 2019

For a few weeks before the bear-chasing incident, Elaine had noticed some changes in Cooper when it was time to relieve himself. He was procrastinating, wanting to go far away off-leash to go, and sometimes he was trying but nothing was happening. It always seemed to resolve itself later, but Elaine had made an appointment with their vet.

At the vet there was concerning news: an enlarged prostate. Prostate infections are fairly common in male dogs, so Cooper was sent home with an antibiotic. Cooper's sensitive tummy could not tolerate the antibiotic. The vet suggested an ultrasound to see if it would reveal what the problem was. The ultrasound was done, some samples were taken, and now everyone was waiting for the results.

It was a Friday afternoon, two days before Cooper's tenth birthday, when Elaine, Allie, and Cooper came up to visit. I didn't know it yet, but they were not bringing good news. We had just sat down to discuss the vet's report, when Cooper left and went out the dog door. Bill happened to be out in the yard, and he noticed that Cooper kept trying to relieve himself, but he couldn't.

While this was going on out back, Elaine and Allie gave me the news: Cooper had an aggressive form of prostate cancer, and there was nothing that could be done for him. There was a mass that was blocking critical elimination functions. They had just finished reading the report in full to me, when Bill came in with the news of what was going on in the back yard.

If he couldn't empty his bladder and his colon, Cooper had to be in terrible pain now. Dogs hide it when they are hurt, so it is difficult to tell, but Cooper was in the air-conditioned house now, yet he was panting. As with Lakota, panting can be a sign of pain with dogs. When this kind of thing happens, we all need to get help assessing our animals' level of discomfort, so we don't let them suffer. The vet had told them nothing could be done to help Cooper, and now he was in crisis. Since he couldn't relieve himself, Cooper had to be in serious misery. Elaine and Allie were struggling. They had very little time to mentally or emotionally prepare themselves to say goodbye to their beloved dog because this had happened so suddenly. Allie said that she had hoped he could make it to his birthday, only two days away. We had planned to have a small celebration and then a larger one, with some dog friends, when the weather cooled down.

A surgeon I know who had a bowel obstruction told me it was a 10 on the pain scale if a kidney stone was an 8. If you can't pee or poop it's not pain—it is agony. And in this case, there was nothing that could be done to fix it. Another look at their boy, unable to relieve himself and struggling, and Elaine and Allie did the unselfish thing: They made the decision to let go of Cooper to avoid him having to suffer. We tearfully agreed that we would all go together. We would take two cars, so each dog would have plenty of room in the back seat, and so neither Elaine nor Allie would have to drive. We were bringing Kaya along with us for a reason.

Back in 2011, as Zeak was nearing the end of his battle with cancer, I had been concerned about Lakota and Cooper. They were so close to Zeak. He was their pack leader and they loved him deeply. I wondered how we should handle it when Zeak departed. So I consulted with a veterinary behaviorist as to how to handle the situation. The behaviorist said to bring all the dogs along when the time came to euthanize Zeakie. I was told to bring the dogs into the examining room when the time came, let them say goodbye, and then remove them from the room when the actual procedure to euthanize was going on. Later, when it was over, they should be brought back into the room and allowed to sniff their deceased friend if they chose to. Just being in the vicinity, they would understand what had happened.

This made sense to me. I off-leashed Lakota on the trails every day. I know that if Zeak were missing, Lakota would not stop searching for him until he found him. I might lose Lakota too, in his quest to find his adopted brother. And Cooper would have been right alongside Lakota searching for The Zeakie Dog. They needed to know what happened to their leader. They had a right to know. And no matter how heartbreaking it was, they needed closure.

Cooper was there when we brought Kaya home. We wanted his calm, gentle energy on hand to greet her and to help her to feel safe. Until the very end, we hiked together almost every day. They played together, Cooper jumping and Kaya chasing him to herd him. He was her only close friend. She needed to know what was happening to her friend. She needed closure. So she was coming with us.

I knew what an agonizing decision this was for Elaine and Allie. Letting go of a terminally ill pet who is about to suffer horribly is a heroic act of unselfish love. The kind of love where you would rather take the hit yourself than let your animal suffer. I had been through this twice in recent years, so I wanted to help all I could, because it hurts, hurts, hurts. I called ahead to let the emergency vets know we would be coming in and why. I gave them all the pertinent information so they could access the vet records, and Elaine and Allie would bring their vet's report with them. Elaine and Allie wanted to call their dog walker and some friends in case they wanted to say goodbye, before we left. I told them to go home and do that and to call us when they were ready. Meanwhile we would prepare our two vehicles with what they needed for the dogs to ride comfortably and safely.

It was about an hour later when they called. We drove down and picked them up. Elaine and Cooper would ride in the bigger SUV, so Elaine could ride in the back seat with her dog. Bill would drive that vehicle. I would drive the other one, with Allie and Kaya riding with me. I was the lead car, and I must have been preoccupied, because I went off course, even though I had made that ride dozens of times. I hooked up my navigator, and it got us where we were going. As we pulled into the parking lot, I briefly felt sick to my stomach. I had been down this road before, and I didn't like where it ended.

We went inside and were quickly ushered into an examining room, since they had all our info logged in. In a few minutes, a vet came in and told us that he would like to take Cooper "in the back" to get a catheter in his leg, and then he would bring him back out where we all could have as much time as we wished with him. Elaine and Allie agreed. That was rightfully their choice, and I don't have a problem with that if the owner is comfortable with it.

I would never agree to this for any dog of my own. I had been through this with Zeak, and I will never again allow myself to be separated from my dog—or my dog to be separated from me—when he or she is dying. Some people may prefer it that way, not wanting to watch their dog get stuck in the leg. For myself, I find separation at that time totally unacceptable and unnecessary.

I am going to digress here to discuss an important matter. I am not a fan of the "in the back" style of veterinary medicine. It is not to benefit the animal or the owner. It is to make things easier for the vet. For years, pet owners have been told that it "makes the dog more nervous if the owner is there." This is misinformation that has been perpetuated forever, and has no basis in fact. The only time it is true is if the owner is so nervous they convey that to their pet, making them more anxious. If the owner is a problem, then that should be addressed on a case-by-case basis. This is the age of information, and many pet owners are savvy, informed people who are capable of handling their animals calmly to help them through exams and procedures. And if that is the case, their animals themselves are calmer, less stressed, and better off in general with their owners with them.

Someone finally did a study on this subject. The National Veterinary School of Alfort in France examined whether a dog's stress level during a veterinary examination was influenced by having their owner present and providing comfort. The authors concluded: "The well-being of dogs during veterinary visits may be improved by affiliative owner-dog interactions."[1]

It is to our dogs' detriment to remove an owner or to remove the dog from the owner, as long as the owner is conducting themselves in an appropriate manner. And if a procedure is so painful that the owner can't bear to see their pet hurt, then it shouldn't be performed without pain control.

There is another reason *some* vets like to bring their patients "in the back": Their patients can't talk. They can be held down, helpless, and have painful procedures and treatments forced on them, without the owner ever knowing it. It saves time and money, but does terrible damage to the poor animal, who not only suffers the pain forcefully inflicted on him, but suffers anxiety every time he or she goes to the vet for the rest of his or her life.

I italicized the word "some" in the above paragraph to emphasize that I do not think this of all vets. I believe most vets are vets because they love animals. But I know it is true of *some* vets. Two vet techs told me the vets they worked for were cruel. I also heard from an

1 Csoltova E., Martineau M., Boissy A, & Gilbert C. "Behavior and physiological reactions in dogs to a veterinary examination: Owner-dog interactions improve canine well-being." *Physiology & Behavior* 2017; 177:270-281.

acquaintance that they took their dog to the vet with a badly broken toenail. Instead of sedating or anesthetizing the dog to perform a surgical procedure, the vet took pliers and ripped the poor animal's nail out with no pain control whatsoever. The dog screamed and knocked the vet on the floor from the excruciating pain he had inflicted on the poor animal. I asked the owner of the pet if he had reported the vet to the state board. He told me he hadn't because the vet was retiring soon. I think the vet should have been charged with animal cruelty.

I am not the only person who feels this way. There are vets who do, and it is giving rise to hundreds of vets converting to "Fear Free" veterinary practices. This is an actual certification that vets can get now. They must adhere to a protocol designed to remove the terror from vet visits—and the insensitivity and, sadly, the cruelty.

It was started by nationally syndicated newspaper columnist and "Good Morning America" contributor Dr. Marty Becker, D.V.M., in response to a lecture by board-certified veterinary behaviorist Dr. Karen Overall. He learned from her that "All of us who deal with animals—including veterinarians, veterinary nurses, trainers, groomers, and boarding personal—are causing repeat, severe, irreversible psychological damage to the animals we care for." Fear free services are gaining popularity because this is the right thing to do. Even the way the office is furnished is considered in this type of animal treatment, with more soft, comforting surfaces.

Loving pet owners have had it with the Neanderthal way their animals are treated by some vets, and demanding more compassionate veterinary care. I am one of them. It took me a while to find a vet that was loving, sensitive, and kind as well as talented and knowledgeable. It was worth the effort to find her for both my dog and me. My dog doesn't like *going* to the vet, but she likes the vet! She kisses her, sits on her lap, and is comfortable enough to take treats there. And I can take my dog to the vet without feeling guilty that I am going to put her through a terrifying ordeal. I know she will have adequate pain and anxiety control when she needs it, and I can help make exams go smoothly by handling my dog and feeding her lots of special, tiny treats, and calming her. All of this is what I consider moving forward. Human medicine has moved past the time when cowboys bit on a stick for anesthesia when they had a bullet removed. We need to move veterinary medicine in the same direction. As my thoughts on needed advances in veterinary compassion concluded, my attention was brought back to the present situation.

The wait for Cooper to come out was seemingly endless—the better part of an hour. When he was finally brought out, he was looking happily drugged and relieved of some or all of his pain. I went over to say goodbye and he smiled at me. I got down and gave him a kiss goodbye and allowed Kaya to sniff him and communicate with him in the wordless way dogs speak to one another. Bill said goodbye, too, and the three of us left Elaine and Allie to have private time with their beloved dog.

We went outside and sat on the front steps of the building. It was a very warm, humid, summer night—exactly what you would expect in New Jersey on the second of August. The last of the great pack was about to depart from the physical world. These three dogs, Lakota, Zeak, and Cooper, had brightened the lives of several thousand people if you were to add together all the people they visited. And the dragon-snake had taken them all: with a vengeance…no mercy. Zeak had waged a fierce battle with it for fifteen months. Lakota had fought for all he was worth, but only lasted two months. And now, it had claimed Cooper's life in what appeared to be weeks. For all of you reading this, I doubt there are many of you who have not been wounded to your core by the loss of a person or animal you love, struck down by this terrible disease.

I have no idea how long it had been when I got a feeling it was over. I didn't want to intrude and ask, so I went in and just discreetly looked into the window. My feeling had been correct. Allie gestured to me to come in. I went back to the door and told Bill to come inside, and the three of us went to the examining room door, opened it, and went in. Cooper was lying in the same position he always assumed by my front door, on the carpet, waiting for his mommies. He looked beautiful, peaceful, and serene. It was very clear from the moment we entered the room that Kaya had known what was going to happen. She was not a bit surprised that Cooper had passed. I am convinced that dogs know more about these happenings than we do.

Elaine and Allie told us that the vet had been very kind and that Cooper had a peaceful, comfortable passing, with his loving family comforting him. They were being very strong, but I knew their hearts were breaking. I also knew the loss would get much worse before it got better. We made arrangements for Cooper to be picked up by a crematorium. Allie and I drove home in semi-silence. I tried to make a little conversation, but Allie and I both knew it was a futile attempt to lift our mood, for truly, there were no words to be said.

Ten days after we brought Cooper's ashes home,
Elaine called to tell me that
Cooper had visited her in a dream.

CHAPTER FORTY-TWO:

Cooper Comes Home: August 8, 2019

On the Thursday following Cooper's passing, Elaine and I set out on the forty-five-minute drive to the crematorium for a private viewing and cremation. I believe that it is helpful for those of us with a close bond to our animals to do this. It is expensive. But it is a comfort and a healing part of the grieving process, just as it is for those of us who lose human family members. It is also the only way to guarantee you will get your own animal's ashes back. Ashes can blow around during group cremations, so there is no guarantee that the ashes you get will be only your animal, and all of your animal.

I was sad for Allie that she couldn't join us because she couldn't get the day off. She needed the comfort of this ceremony. I told her I would go with Elaine and give her support; we would bring Cooper's ashes home, where they belonged.

It is finally beginning to be recognized that the loss of a pet who is a closely bonded member of your family is every bit as painful as losing a human member of your family. People who are grieving the loss of their pets are in need of help with the grieving process. It can cause all sorts of lingering problems from depression to PTSD. It's a shame that some employers are not up to speed on this. It can make it more difficult and do real damage.

The crematorium was also a cemetery for pets, and was situated on acres of beautiful rolling hills. They even had grief counselors for people who needed help with their loss. There were beautiful statues of animals, flowers, and a serene, peaceful setting. We entered the home-like building and walked into a room appointed like a living room. As soon as we walked into the room, the lights turned on, and, seconds later, a woman entered and greeted us warmly and offered her condolences. She ushered us into an office and explained what would transpire. First, she entered names and information into a computer and asked how Elaine wanted the information on the cremation certificate. We discussed a few other things, and then she told us to bring our car around and to follow her car up to the top of the hill where the crematorium was located.

When we arrived, we parked and got out of our vehicle. It was a beautiful, sunny, warm day with blue skies nestled into the green, rolling hills. Our host brought us into a small room where the viewing was to be. She told us we would be alone with Cooper's body for about twenty minutes, and then she would check with us to see if we were ready to leave.

Cooper was lying in a very natural position, a blanket with pawprints covering his lower half. We had been told we could remove the blanket if we wished. I had brought three roses: one for Elaine, one for Allie, and one for us. We laid them alongside his body, his beautiful black fur glistening under the lights. The tears flowed and I was glad for the box of tissues that were provided. Elaine and I talked about the great times our three dogs had together, the wonderful work they had done, and how blessed we were to have our lives touched by such loving spirits.

Then we said our tearful goodbyes. Elaine waited outside. No matter how sad I was about losing Cooper, I knew it did not compare to the heartbreak of his owners. It was too hard for Elaine to watch, so I witnessed the body going into the cremation chamber alone. As I did with my own dogs, I wanted to be sure of what was done with our dogs' remains. As I mentioned before, there are cruel and unscrupulous people in this world. I always make sure two vets confirm my dog is indeed deceased. I was told at the emergency vet's that they routinely have two vets confirm an animal's passing after they are euthanized. It is a good safeguard. Then I follow his or her remains from start to finish. The most important part of this is to be sure your dog is completely euthanized. You don't want your suffering dog to be sedated, wake up, and fall into the wrong hands.

We were told it would take about two and a half hours for Cooper's ashes to be ready for us, so we drove to a nearby restaurant and had a long, slow lunch. We reminisced about the days of the great pack: Dogs running through the woods so hard we could feel it in the earth beneath our feet, hiking with the snow swirling around us as the dogs tore through the white powder, and hot summer days at the dog beach. We killed some time poking through the stores in the craft village nearby, and then headed back to pick up Cooper's ashes.

When we arrived, they were ready for us. The woman who had helped us when we arrived came out of a side door and handed us a wooden box with Cooper's ashes. As she held the box, Elaine commented that they were still warm. We got into the SUV, drove down the hill, and started the trip back to bring Cooper's remains home, where they belonged.

Ten days after we brought Cooper's ashes home, Elaine called to tell me that Cooper had visited her in a dream. She recounted him running toward her with his ears down and happy to see her. He laid his head on the couch and she could see the white hairs on his chin. As I have mentioned before, in my experience, there is a distinct difference between a dream visit from a spirit and an ordinary dream. The visit is in high definition. It is sharp and clear and colorful and often multisensory. When Elaine told me she could see the white hairs on his chin, I was convinced that this was a visit. It is easiest for our beloved departed ones to visit us in a dream because our brains are in a very receptive state then. Not everyone is wired to be able to receive in this way, but enough of us are that we can't all be imagining it! I was so glad that Cooper had found his way to come through to Elaine.

It was a familiar muzzle doing what it had done so many times when Cooper was with her in the physical world.

CHAPTER FORTY-THREE:

Elaine's Visit from Cooper: September 2019

Since Cooper had passed away over the summer, the children at the school where he served as a therapy dog did not know he was gone. Cooper visited two special education classes at this particular school. Elaine had contacted the teacher of the one class and told her about the dog's passing, but the other class's instructor was no longer there. The teacher Elaine had contacted had invited Elaine to come in. The children had made cards for Elaine and the teacher thought it would help them to see Elaine and talk about the dog they had come to look forward to seeing.

Elaine brought along a collage of photos of Cooper for this class and the other class that they could hang on their bulletin boards. She entered the first class and spent some time talking with the children and answering their questions about what had happened to Cooper. When the visit to that class had come to an end, Elaine went to the next room to deliver the poster and explain to the children why Cooper wouldn't be able to visit any more.

She knocked on the door and the new teacher beckoned her to come in. A very withdrawn boy who had been huddled in a corner of the room called out Cooper's name and ran towards Elaine. When he saw that she was alone, he asked her where Cooper was. She told him and the rest of the class that Cooper had become ill and had passed away over the summer. She had come to explain why he wouldn't be visiting anymore and to bring some pictures for them. The boy who had run toward her now turned around and went back to the corner he had been in when she entered and huddled there, obviously deeply saddened by the loss of the dog he had so enjoyed visiting with.

Therapy dogs have the ability to transform the mood of the people they visit to a degree that is very surprising. I have heard from people many times that a few minutes with a therapy dog can lift their mood for an entire day. These kids were going to miss their visits with Cooper. Elaine had done the right thing visiting the children and answering their questions, but it had been difficult for her. It had only been a few weeks since Cooper's passing and she was grieving. Keeping her composure and handling the children's questions and comments had been emotionally taxing.

Elaine had been dealing for some time with health issues that required medical intervention. One of them required intravenous medications at regular intervals. She had also had a lot of bloodwork done recently, so she was heading to her doctor with a sore arm and was not looking forward to being stabbed again and sitting for an infusion with a needle in her arm. The fact that she was grieving the loss of her beloved dog compounded the fact that she didn't want to be going for this treatment, but it was not something she could skip.

She arrived at the doctor's office and was ushered to the recliner where she would be administered her medication. She felt the nasty pinch of the needle on her already sore arm and settled back to wait for the slow drip to enter her body. She was feeling down, beaten up, and tired. She tried to relax, hoping to drift off to sleep when something abruptly awakened her.

Her arm was resting propped on a pillow as it had been many times before for this procedure. But something unseen was making its presence known: A warm muzzle, complete with whiskers, was pressing into her resting hand. It was a familiar muzzle doing what it had done so many times when Cooper was with her in the physical world. She knew exactly what it was the moment she felt it, but was stunned, elated, and filled with joy as she realized her boy had come through to her to comfort her at this time when she was feeling so vulnerable, sad, and weary. She had thought she would never feel that again. Happily, she had just discovered that she had been mistaken!

"As I had thought, I saw her image,
standing on the bed, wagging at me---as if to say,
I'm all better now, Mom, and I can
jump up here all by myself again!'"

CHAPTER FORTY-FOUR:

Ainsley: December 2019

There are those among us, such as the person in the "Animal Endangerment" chapter of this book, who have little regard for animals—are lacking in compassion, empathy, and respect for them. And there are those who can love only the perfect: the perfect show dog, from the perfect breeder, with the perfect bloodlines. But there are also those among us who are capable of opening their hearts and souls with a magnitude of love that is uplifting to all of us who love animals. Such is the story of Ainsley.

I first met Valerie Kerwin at a fundraiser for a rescue group. It was the Christmas season, and she was donating her time taking pet photographs for people to benefit the rescue. She took a picture of Kaya and me and did a lovely job—it was clear she did beautiful work that was a cut above the usual pet photo. We had that instant connection that I experience with people who deeply love animals. She is also a friend of my friend, Donna.

Since I wrote *Walking with the Shadow of Love,* I have sought out people who have had incidents of afterlife contact with their pets. I only accept incidents for my books from people I know personally, or people who are known to be trustworthy by people I know. So I was delighted when Valerie had a story to tell about her Chinese Crested dog, Ainsley. Before I heard about her afterlife contacts from her dog, I wanted to know how Valerie came to rescue—and I do mean rescue in every sense of the word—Ainsley.

Valerie and her partner, Liz, had four dogs: three Corgis, and a Chinese Crested. They were not looking to expand their family with another dog. And while Valerie loved her powderpuff Chinese Crested (there are two types of Chinese Crested dogs: the powder-puff, which has a thick fur coat, and the hairless variety), she was not drawn to the hairless variety of that breed, so she didn't particularly want one. But when a dog wants to find its way to you, it is a force of nature and an act of God, and cannot be denied.

Local dog breeders know one another, and a breeder that Valerie knew had become aware of a dog in trouble: It was in the clutches of an irresponsible breeder of these hairless dogs. It was not show quality, and therefore was unwanted and was being neglected. She suggested Valerie give this dog a home. Valerie and Liz agreed to go see this dog...unenthusiastically. When they arrived at the breeder's, this, in Valerie's own words, is what followed:

"When we parked in front of what appeared to be a pleasant home, in a nice neighborhood, we could see a dog on the back porch. It was November of 2003, and bitterly cold that night. We went inside, and I will not describe the interior, other than to say that it was shockingly unlike what the exterior promised. The breeder (who is no longer involved in the breed and was not respected by her peers) led us into the cellar to wait, while she processed the sale of a clean and perky puppy to a young couple. As I sat there, she dumped a filthy, shivering creature into my lap, to meet—she was calling her 'spider.' The poor thing curled up tight against me, and within seconds, my heart melted, and I knew she wasn't staying there another minute.

The breeder came over a few minutes later, and threw out a ridiculous figure for the dog, before turning back to see the other couple to the door. I hissed into Liz's ear, 'Write the check!' She looked at me rather stunned, because I was the financially responsible member of our partnership, and she knew how I felt about hairless dogs. I whispered again, 'Write the check!!' She pulled out the checkbook, and in fifteen minutes we were on the way home.

The puppy slept in my lap the entire way home, until—literally a minute from my driveway—she lifted her head and delicately puked into my hand. Rather than being horrified, my heart just burst a little more and I knew it was 'true love.'

Years later, when Liz and I separated, Ainsley was the only dog to come with me. She was my 'heart dog,' and moved with me into my parents' home, where I still live with my mother. In December of 2014, she was diagnosed with liver cancer and underwent successful surgery. The following year, routine follow-up testing revealed she had Leukemia. She was given a seventy percent chance of living two more years. With medical treatment, the two years stretched into four, with a good quality of life, but the medication took a toll on her GI tract. So my mom started cooking a bland chicken diet for her.

The last few months of her life, she became very weak, and I carried her up and down the stairs and, outside to go to the bathroom frequently, as her kidneys began to fail. She slept on a soft dog bed, on my bed, safe between me and the wall, so she couldn't fall off, under her special 'blankie.' Each morning I carried her, still in her bed, downstairs, to spend the day in the living room with her Grandma, while I went to work.

In the last few weeks, I would feed her by hand as she lay in my lap. She stopped eating on Christmas Day. I knew that was the sign I had dreaded, and called the vet to make the appointment. She crossed the Rainbow Bridge on Friday, December twenty-seventh, two thousand nineteen. I was with her until the very end."

As I read the account of Ainsley's life that Valerie had sent me, I was moved by how blessed Ainsley was to find such a devoted, loving home. There were some similarities to how Zeak found his way to me: How we instantly experienced this tremendous bond, the especially, deep, loving relationship we had, and our long hard battle with cancer. It also made me recall the powerful light path that pulled me to Kaya. It made me ponder something I have often thought about: the miracle of how and why our animals find their way to us. Why this particular dog or cat? Why that particular person? I can feel the answer to my core: None of this is an accident.

The loss of an animal that you have a deep bond with is devastation of a magnitude that no one sees coming until it hits you. But Ainsley's story does not end with her passing, and Valerie kept a journal at the time and recorded the events that followed. Again, in her own words, Valerie continued her story:

"The first time Ainsley came to see me was in a dream on January twenty-seventh, two thousand twenty, which was one month to the day of her passing. This was my journal entry: 'I dreamt that Mom's Christmas tree was still up and lit, but had no ornaments. My sisters were visiting, and someone asked about the star on top, so I started downstairs to get it. One of my sisters called out to me to watch out, because Ainsley was following me down the stairs. I turned on the stairs, and there she was! I picked her up and she was so heavy—full of life, not thin and frail. At the bottom of the stairs I put her down, and she ran around me wagging her tail, as I told her how much I missed her. She was very happy and restored to full health and energy. I woke up sad, but also happy! I think it was her telling me that she is really OK now.

The next day I took down my own Christmas tree, saving an ornament with Ainsley's picture on it for last. It was hard to let go of my last holiday season with Ainsley. That ornament is in my bedroom, hanging over her ashes."

Valerie's dream contained something that I have noticed in my own dream visits: It was multisensory. She not only *saw* Ainsley in her dream, but she *felt* her weight. My dream visits are distinguished from regular dreams by their incredible sharpness, and the fact that they are often multisensory. They are also usually lucid dreams: I am aware I am dreaming, as Valerie seemed to be, because she told Ainsley how much she missed her; so she was aware of her passing.

In *Walking with the Shadow of Love,* I tell of a neighbor's experience, feeling his dog in bed with him, after the dog had passed. I have also experienced that, and now, Valerie describes her experience with this type of visit:

"I have experienced contact from Ainsley, and my mother says she sees her out of the corner of her eye, frequently. I have felt her in bed with me in 'her spot.' She pushed against me with her feet like she used to do, and then shifted so her back was against mine. I was awake and could even hear the covers rustling. It was so real, I reached my hand behind me; absolutely certain she would be there.

I have numerous photos of Ainsley around the edge of the dresser mirror in my room. One keeps falling in the night and waking me. It's a silly picture of Ainsley, wearing sunglasses. I bought them because I thought they were a good idea, and she did not care for them. I wonder if she's getting back at me for making her wear them.

One of my friends gifted me with a soft, little throw blanket for Ainsley for a Christmas gift. I keep it on the foot of my bed. On March twenty-fifth, two thousand twenty, after I had made the bed in the morning and gone to brush my teeth, I returned to the bedroom to find the corner of the blanket turned back like it might have been if she'd jumped up on the bed by herself. As I had that thought, I saw her image, standing on the bed, wagging at me—as if to say, 'I'm all better now, Mom, and I can jump up here all by myself again!'"

Valerie's sharing of Ainsley's story with me led her to seek out the company of a deeply trusted friend—who has also had visits from animal companions, as well as from her grandfather. When she arrived at her friend's house, Valerie discovered that her friend had also had a dream visit from Ainsley. This part of the story illustrates how our loved ones want us to live our lives, and love again, and how they try to help us heal so we can do that. Valerie wrote to me:

"This is the dream that my friend recounted to me, which she had about four nights ago, which would have been dur-

ing the time when I was really thinking about my Ainsley, and writing to you:

She dreamt that a dog approached her...a dog that she 'knew' but couldn't name in the dream. It looked like a 'hairless Chihuahua' with hair on its head. It told her that it was lost and couldn't find its way over the Rainbow Bridge because it still had its leash on. Valerie's friend looked down and, yes, there was a bright pink leash, which was how she knew the dog was a girl. She asked the dog if she wanted her to cut the leash, and the dog said 'yes.' Valerie's friend pulled a pair of scissors from her pocket—the huge kind that are used for ribbon-cutting ceremonies—and cut the leash. The dog said, 'Say goodbye to her for me' and then, Valerie's friend felt the love that the dog had for Valerie. When she woke up, she knew it was Ainsley sending a message to Valerie.

We both started crying as she told me about the dream. We discussed it and concluded that Ainsley must have chosen her to deliver her message because she knew that she was one of the very few people in my life with absolute credibility. She has offered me wisdom and been a support during the most trying days of Ainsley's illnesses, and suffered her own share of heartbreaking losses.

When Ainsley first passed, my friend had mentioned getting another dog and I told her I wasn't nearly ready to even consider it, and she never mentioned it again. But today, after hearing her dream, I do think that it is time to start looking.

So, you see, I went up there today to figure out what more I wanted you to know about my Ainsley, and my Ainsley sent me a clear and simple message that I was not able to receive on my own—through another person. Ainsley has written the end of her story, all on her own.

Thank you, so much. If I hadn't started this little journey with you, I'm quite certain I would not have found myself at the end. Not that it's the 'end.' Because I know I will see Ainsley again—and maybe soon—as it's also a beginning, and I know she wants it this way."

And that, is Ainsley's…and Valerie's story.

The locksmith and his wife had one child:
a son named Matthew, who was
a kind and loving boy and
a joy to everyone around him.
Every day he told his parents he loved them
and hugged them.

CHAPTER FORTY-FIVE:

See You Again: January 2020

In the years since I wrote *Walking with the Shadow of Love,* I have encountered numerous people who have had afterlife contacts with their beloved ones—both four-legged and two-legged—who have passed on. People are often reluctant to open up such things until someone else shares that they have had this kind of experience because they fear the unkind judgments of skeptics.

The scientific and medical communities have not helped this. In her book *The Empath's Survival Guide,* which I spoke of in the Introduction, psychiatrist Judith Orloff, M.D., states, "Medicine too often pathologizes anything 'different' that it doesn't understand."

I puzzle at why they are so sure of themselves, even though they are so often wrong. (This week eggs are good for us. Next week they cause heart attacks and clog arteries.) Since I am an open book—literally—about these matters, many people share their stories with me. I am amazed by the sheer number of people who have had such contacts from loved ones. I think they are even more common than we think, because some people don't recognize these communications for what they are. One of these stories came to me recently in an indirect but very intriguing way. It is indicative of how, even in the midst of tragedy, our animal friends are there to love and support us...to lift us up at our moments of deepest despair.

I have known my mechanic for many years. Our mothers used to ride horses together. Early in my teaching career he was one of my students. When I drop off and pick up my car, we always have something to talk about, and he knows of my connection with animals and the remarkable experience that moved me to write *Walking with the Shadow of Love*. So it got my attention when he told me there was a story I would be interested in, about a family in town and a spiritual experience they had with their dog, in the context of a devastating family loss. He gave me a name and phone number and suggested I call. He told me that the man, who happened to be a locksmith, would be expecting the call.

The holidays came and went—I didn't want to disturb a family during the holidays and I was too busy to be writing anyway—so it was the second week in January when I called the number on the slip of paper. The man who answered remembered who I was when I mentioned my mechanic's name. We spoke briefly and he agreed to get back to me as soon as he caught up with some work he had to do. I could tell he was having a very difficult time talking about his loss, and I silently wondered if he would ever call me back, knowing I was interested in telling his story in a book I was writing. But a few days later he did call back and made an appointment for him and his wife to come to our home to tell me their story. Their story revolved around the tragic loss of their son from cancer at twenty-nine years of age, and something that happened as he was dying, regarding their dog. Since this dog had died years earlier, I was very interested to find out exactly what had happened. The couple arrived right on time and, after introductions and offers of refreshments, we sat down to talk.

I explained that, while I wanted to tell their story, due to the loss they had incurred I also wanted them to be comfortable with what they were about to share. I went over some technical things about signing a release at some point, and told them I would send them what I had written and they could decide after reading it if they were comfortable with me using the material.

As they began to tell their story, I could feel the pain and devastation of the loss weighing their every word. It was also apparent that the woman had been able to make some progress in processing her loss, but the man was really struggling. Some of this was probably because he had not only lost his son, but also his mother only five months before. Their story is as follows:

The locksmith and his wife had one child: a son named Matthew, who was a kind and loving boy and a joy to everyone around him. Every day he told his parents he loved them and hugged them.

When Matt was around nine years old, his mother was delivering an order to a customer who had a dilemma: She had bought a German Shepherd puppy after getting permission from her landlord. Soon after she got the puppy, the landlord changed his mind and said he didn't want any pets in his building. She was desperately trying to find a home for the dog, and asked Matt's mother if she knew anyone who would adopt this puppy. Matt's mother spoke to her husband about it, and they came to meet the puppy. They knew the minute they laid eyes on it that it was going to be their dog. They took the puppy home, and it also bonded instantly with their son, Matt. They named the puppy Daisy, and like their son, the dog was a blessing and a joyful addition to their family.

Daisy was the locksmith's "Velcro dog," and followed him everywhere. She grew to be a big—120 pound—lovely and gentle dog. She adored their son and watched over him like the good shepherd she was. She could be out in the yard with no fence, and just stayed within her perimeters. It was clear that she was where she belonged—where she had been meant to be from the beginning. She was a loyal and loving member of their family, and Matt grew up with Daisy as his cherished companion. When it came Daisy's time to depart the physical world, the whole family was devastated. There is just no way of knowing the agony of losing an animal that you are deeply bonded with until it happens to you. It blindsides you and leaves a wound that never entirely heals.

Around the time of Daisy's passing, Matt had started working for UPS. He worked for them for several years, but had a strong desire to be an electrician. So he started taking classes to that end. He was in his mid-twenties and had just bought his first vehicle, a milestone for any young person. He had a close and loving relationship with his parents and was looking forward to achieving his goal of finishing school and becoming an electrician.

About halfway through 2016 Matt became aware of a pain in his groin. Since he was working for UPS, nobody thought it was anything other than something he had pulled lifting a heavy package. But the pain didn't go away, and when it failed to resolve itself in a reasonable amount of time, he saw a doctor. No one in the family was prepared for the news that the doctor gave them…a diagnosis of testicular cancer. He was the picture of robust health. He was twenty-seven years old. How do you wrap your head around such a diagnosis? And in that moment, all of their lives were changed forever.

What followed was a two-year-long battle with a relentless foe. The family travelled to New York to find the best doctors at the best hospital. They were propelled onto the awful roller coaster ride that is the battle with cancer: surgery, hope, then finding out that it had spread; treatments, hope, then finding out that they had not worked. Matt was enduring miserable nine and ten hour chemotherapy treatments. He suffered through all of this because of what it offered: a chance. Matt did not want to end what he had just begun, that being his life. He wanted to live and he was willing to fight for it.

A year and seven months into the war with cancer, Matt's father lost his mother. Any time is a difficult time to lose one's mother, but this was even worse than one could imagine—because Matt's parents were struggling with their son's illness. And so, the locksmith said goodbye to his mother while continuing to try to save the life of his son.

A short time after his mother's death, Matt's father walked into the living room one night to a familiar sight. It was his mother. She was sitting on the couch—a ray of light illuminating her—doing the crossword puzzle she did all the time when she was living. Then she got up and walked over to her son and hugged him. Her stunned son told her he missed her. She said she was there to visit Matt. "Matt has cancer," the locksmith said to her.

"I know." she said. "I'll take care of him." With that, she disappeared, leaving her son in a state of mixed emotions, trying to sort out both the joy and the shock of seeing her, and wondering what she meant by, "I'll take care of him."

The next five months were completely consumed with trying to save Matt's life. At times, it would look like the brutal treatments—chemotherapy and radiation—were making progress, and they would have hope—elation—joy. Then the cancer would resurge and the hope, elation, and joy would be shattered again. When his parents looked discouraged, Matt would tell them to smile. During this time, Matt had a song he loved and listened to often: "See You Again" by Charlie Puth.

At the end of the five months, the unrelenting treatment regimen had taken its toll on Matt. The doctors informed Matt's mother there was nothing more they could do to help him, and then they—along with Matt's mother—told Matt. Matt was devastated. He told them he wanted to go home.

Home. Hospital Bed. Hospice. Morphine. His parents were now keeping a bedside vigil. They knew it would not be long. Matt was being maintained on morphine to ease his pain. It was a quiet vigil. There was no more war, no battles left…just waiting. It was on the fifth night that the waiting was to end.

In a sudden burst, Matt was awake and waving his arms and legs so violently that his father ran to his side to hold him to keep him from injuring himself by striking his arms on the bed frame. His mother stuffed pillows around him to cushion his head, and in a while Matt calmed down and rested. His mother kept a vigil on the coach next to him and dozed off.

It was two hours later that his mother was awakened. She noticed that Matt's breathing had slowed. She sat by him and held his hand and told him she was there with him. His mother, knowing in her heart that her son needed to hear it, did the most unselfish thing a mother could possibly do: told him that it was OK to let go. Then she ran to get her husband to tell him that she thought Matt was taking his last breaths. And then, as though he had been waiting to be released in that way, Matthew left the physical world, reaching out and calling a name—over and over and over.

He adored his mother, but that was not who he called as he left this earth. He had a close, loving relationship with his father—but that was not who he called. They were not going where he was going because it was not their time for this journey now. It wasn't even his grandmother, who had visited to say she would take care of him, but wasn't the one who had come to help him cross over from this world to the next. The name he was calling out was a name from years past. But there was no mistaking who had come for Matt—come to escort him from this life to the next—because he called the name out again, and again, and again: Daisy! Daisy! Daisy!

Weeks passed in the blur that accompanies a devastating loss. If one is fortunate enough to fall asleep, he or she always wakes up with the first thought in his or her mind being the loss...sometimes wondering if this is real or some terrible nightmare. But on one particular morning, Matt's mother was awakened to the sound of her son's voice calling to wake her up. She had been sleeping, and the sound woke her up, and was such a shock that it left her in a state of confusion.

First, she wondered if she had dreamed it. Second, she remembered hearing her son wake her up many times, but he always called her the same way: He called her twice, always twice. But this time, she had only heard him call her once. Had she imagined it? A few minutes later, she had answers to her questions.

Her husband, who had been sleeping in a different room, came in to give her some exciting news: He had heard their son calling his mother to wake her up. But the locksmith had not been sound asleep. He had been awake; plagued with the insomnia he'd had since Matt had passed. Since he was not sound asleep, he heard their son call to wake his mother up as he always had…twice. Both of them—in different rooms—had heard the sound of their son calling his mother. Matt's mom had just slept through the first one.

Daisy adored their son and watched over him like the good shepherd she was.

The words being spoken---
in some silent form of communication---
were, "Bowie's flying."

EPILOGUE:

In the Eye of the Storm: February 2020

On February eleventh of 2020, my "BFF" Sandra went to the hospital for a routine test. Before the test she was asked a bunch of the questions someone is usually asked before such visits. But then she was asked two questions she found surprising. First, she was asked if she had traveled out of the country in the last year. Second, she was asked if she had travelled to China in the past year.

We were having some quality girlfriend time, over lattes, when she told me about this. We had both had different kinds of tests over the years, but neither one of us had ever been asked such questions. That was how, later on, we knew that *they knew*...they knew in early February about the real threat from the novel Corona virus possibly coming here. They weren't telling us, yet, to take precautions, but they knew. We briefly passed over the subject and moved on to more fun discussions, for we had no idea what lay ahead.

We were making plans as we caffeinated ourselves. My seventy-fifth birthday was coming up in a few months, and we always celebrated our birthdays together—especially milestone ones. The plan was to go to a local day spa and get a massage, then go out for a long, slow lunch together. We always cherished these special times together. We had been friends for a long way down our roads and always had a lot of memories to share and new ones to make together.

Sandra had two cats. They were both getting on in years. The male, named Bowie, after singer David Bowie, was twenty years old. The female, named Lizzie, was eighteen. Both had been having health issues on and off, but both were hanging in there. It was back in January, right around the time that the news of the existence of a new and dangerous virus in China was coming out, that Bowie began to fail. There had been several trips to the vet, and Sandra was preparing herself for the worst.

One afternoon, Sandra and Lizzie were at home, standing at the bottom of the stairs, ready to go up. Bowie was upstairs. However, Sandra was stopped in her tracks at the bottom because she heard words—silent words that she heard in her ears and her head—and she knew they were coming from Lizzie. The words being spoken—in some silent form of communication—were, "Bowie's flying." Sandra quickly climbed the stairs, only to find Bowie sleeping in the bedroom.

"What just happened here?" she wondered? When she called me to talk about it, I shared that I had seen my dogs "out of their bodies" once or twice, when they were sleeping. I also mentioned the dream visit I had with Lakota, where he took me on a little journey through my house when I was sleeping. I told her that Lizzie might be preparing her for Bowie getting ready to leave his body permanently…soon.

That turned out to be the case. Soon after that incident, Bowie took a turn for the worst. Sandra and her husband took their beloved pet to the vet. The vet told them there was nothing more that could be done, and that the kind thing would be to help Bowie out of his body with euthanasia. They said goodbye to Bowie just as the pandemic exploded in New York and New Jersey, and we were all ordered to stay in our homes and "shelter in place."

Sandra was broken-hearted and turned to Lizzie for comfort. We were all stressed out and terrified of the deadly virus that was spreading like a wildfire. Sandra and I both had asthma. Sandra had two parents in their nineties to care for. She was helping them to stay in their own home, following their wishes. How could she do that and "shelter in place?"

In addition to asthma, I also had coronary disease, high blood pressure, and a messed-up digestive system that literally could not tolerate most medications to the point of gastritis and ulcers. I was the poster child for the person the virus would kill. We both took the restrictions very seriously. I was worried that the grieving process would lower Sandra's immune system's resistance. We both had always kept a good stock of supplies at home, after several bad storms had left us stranded for a week or so. So we stayed home, listening to the daily accounts of the ferocious battle that was raging in our hospitals—a battle so fierce that they were having trouble finding room for all the casualties of this war with an unseen enemy. We could feel the horrible suffering going on all around us. It felt like we were in the eye of a terrible storm, and while we were safe, if we moved at all we would be pulled into it. So

*Meanwhile, Sandra's Bowie was seeing to it that
she had support from him,
even though he had just departed
from the physical world.*

we froze in place, and said prayers of gratitude that we were blessed to be sheltered from it. Sandra shuttled back and forth from her home to her parents' home, keeping them supplied and checking on their needs.

Meanwhile, Sandra's Bowie was seeing to it that she had support from him, even though he had just departed from the physical world. Sandra had experienced contacts from departed loved ones before. She was clairaudient, meaning she could *hear* messages from the world of spirits. As she was walking by the coffee table in her great room, she heard an unfamiliar sound. She followed the sound to a candle with a "Love" charm attached to it. The charm was rattling, producing the sound she heard. It had never done that before and has not done it since that day. It was located next to the chair that she and Bowie sat in every evening, with him in her arms.

The next day, as she walked into the library, she noticed a beam of sunlight shining on Bowie's favorite chair, as well as on the spot in front of the fireplace where he would lie down every night. As she approached the sunlight, she heard a message: "Look for me in this chair, Mommy. I love you Mommy. Don't look by the heat grate where I was so sick—don't look there."

The next afternoon at four p.m. she heard his nails clicking on the hardwood floors—just as she always had at that time when he was alive. She looked out on the lawn and there were doves and a blue jay there. Sandra's husband was a veteran who had been killed in the Vietnam war. He was a helicopter pilot who died trying to save his fellow soldiers. His name was Jay, and he always sent her blue jays at times he wanted to connect or communicate with her. She had also received clairaudient messages from him at various times over the years. This time the message was delivered in a song: David Bowie's "Learning to Fly" came on the radio. She has since heard feline Bowie deliver the message himself: "I'm flying, Mommy!"

Over the next few weeks, Sandra felt Bowie's presence with her many times. Rainbows appeared everywhere in her home, with a startling frequency, and in places that they had never appeared before and had no apparent reason to be. A month after his passing—just an hour short of the exact time of his passing, she heard his collar bell in the kitchen, just like she used to when he was alive in the physical world. A song she always sang to him came on the TV right after she had just finished singing it to Lizzie. And one morning, as she was sitting at her makeup table, the light blinked on and off and she heard a message: It was from her aunt who had passed away a few years earlier. Her aunt told her, "I have Bowie."

While Sandra was going through the loss of her beloved pet and the shock of dealing with the pandemic, my anxiety was skyrocketing and my blood pressure climbing to unsafe heights. My anxiety issue goes back to an incident when I was six or seven years old where I experienced a brief period of suffocation, due to a very large nurse sitting on me to hold me down, while I had stitches in my arm and leg without any local anesthesia (so much for "the good old days"). There is a window at six or seven years of age, where—if trauma is experienced—it is difficult to ever extinguish, even much later in life. All of my claustrophobia issues are actually a fear of suffocation. They are serious and paralyzing, and the invasion of a virus that suffocated people to death was not helping me one bit.

One night, I fell asleep in my chair in front of the TV—something that was not uncommon. But what woke me up was an uncommon, but very welcome event: a full, solid, visual image of Lakota. He was lying on the right arm of my chair, which was a location he had visited me at before. If he were in a body, it would have been impossible for him to perch there, because he was much too big. But his spirit body just floated there beside me. I always get a rush of energy and strength when I have a contact from one of my boys. I really needed it this time, and Lakota knew it, so he was here to help me. It was a much-needed blessing, and it would strengthen me for the days ahead.

Two weeks later, near the time of my birthday, I again saw Lakota. This time he was walking across my living room, his long otter tail waving behind him. I really needed comforting right then, and it was such a blessing to have these contacts.

Kaya is a source of joy and strength, too. She is such a good dog and makes everything easy for me, which I really need right here and now. Anything I ask of her, she does for me. She is loving and adorable and loves to play with me, which cheers me up in these very troubling times. She is intelligent and incredibly calm, which amazes me after what she has gone through. I am just stunned that such a wonderful dog could have been treated so badly and abandoned. I just can't imagine how such cruelty can inhabit the human race.

Because Kaya had come so far, I decided she deserved a chance to achieve the same honor that Lakota and Zeak had: So I signed her up to take the American

Kennel Club Canine Good Citizen test. Due to the pandemic, we were taking the test outside with masks on. At one point in the test, Kaya had to hold a down/stay, while other dogs were walked past her in close proximity. She had to stay and the leash had to be slack—in other words, she had to stay on her own. One of the dogs in the group was very unruly and predatory. A dog like this would not normally be allowed in the same class as the test class, but the pandemic was causing classes to be combined. This dog was being walked past Kaya, just a few feet away, when it launched into a lunging, snarling, barking frenzy directed at her. The dog's handler had her hands full getting the dog past Kaya. Not many dogs would have held their position in the face of such an onslaught. But Kaya did, demonstrating how brave she was to the amazement of everyone there. She passed her test with flying colors, despite a challenge most dogs never have to face in this test, dazzling the evaluator. She has truly come a million miles for me, and I am so blessed and so grateful to have such a great dog. To accomplish this, she had to give me the hardest thing I ever asked of her: trust.

And so, as we face an uncertain future, our beloved animals—both here and on the other side—are letting us know that they are here to comfort us and give us strength. Sandra's contacts are more clairaudient and mine are more clairvoyant. But sometimes we do get contacts through other senses as well, even smell. We also get contacts from beloved people who have departed, but we get contacts from our animals much more frequently and they are stronger, louder, clearer, and sharper. I think they connect with us differently on a soul level and it is easier for them to reach us.

I have nine friends who have had contacts from spirits—eight of us mostly from our animals, and one who has only had contact with human spirits. Neither I nor any of my friends has any control over when we get these "visits." Many, but not all, people have experienced these blessings. I suspect it is the way our brains are wired, but I really don't know why everyone has not had these occurrences. I also know that some people, who love their animals with all their hearts, haven't had contacts. Or perhaps they have, but they haven't recognized them for what they are. I feel the frustration of those who wish they could have these experiences, and have not *yet* been able to connect. It has nothing to do with deserving this: Some of the best people I know can't connect. All I can do is share what I and others have experienced, so they have the comfort of knowing their beloved pet companions are OK, and pray for the portal to open for them in the future.

At this writing, I have no idea if we will ever return to the normal we once knew. A vaccine as effective as the polio vaccine could flip things back to the way they were, but there is some question whether that can happen with this type of virus. My prayer is that this huge hit to our way of life, which is happening worldwide, will wake up the human race to the cruelty we are inflicting on one another and on the animal species with which we share this planet. If that happens and if we are capable of changing ourselves, maybe this pandemic, which has caused such pain and loss, will have resulted in some good as well.

But whatever the fate of the human race, those of us blessed with these contacts from beyond the Rainbow Bridge know our animals are still in existence in a different form. They are with us to guide and help us, and will be there when it is time for us to trade this form of being for a new kind of existence…free to "fly" with our precious, beloved, and profoundly missed animal spirits.

But Kaya did, demonstrating how brave she was
to the amazement of everyone there.

ABOUT THE AUTHOR

Margo Bowblis has had a deep love for animals her entire life—literally since she was a toddler. Her mother, being very traditional, was frustrated by her daughter's lack of interest in dolls and desire to play only with toy animals. Margo bonded closely with her first dog and had a favorite pony she loved to ride at a local stable. While she loved all animals, dogs and horses were her favorites.

This love of animals led to an interest in art, and portraying the beauty of animals. The author pursued a career in art education, and graduated from Montclair State College in New Jersey with a degree in Fine Arts and a Teaching Certification. She married, had a son, and enjoyed teaching art in middle school. She acquired two Labrador Retrievers that she did obedience work with, because she loved working with dogs. She felt it enhanced her bond with them and thought of it as communication, rather than training.

As time passed, life's responsibilities took her time and energy away from her passion for animals. She enjoyed teaching and really dug in, trying new ways to get students to engage with art, develop skills in it, and even a passion for it. She believes that art is universal, can connect with any other interests in life, and is a central part of a complete education. In 1989, she received the New Jersey Governor's Award for her work in the field of education. In 1990 she received a grant from the Geraldine Dodge Foundation to study the creative process. She taught until 1998, when a bout with the flu left her with a prolonged illness that forced her to retire. She was later diagnosed with fibromyalgia syndrome, migraines, and chronic fatigue syndrome. She spent six months unable to get out of her bed or recliner.

She started to gradually do a little more each day, and saw her condition improve very slowly. She also found medication that helped the migraines. But she felt something was missing in her life, and realized that working and family responsibilities had forced her to give up what she most loved. She got a Labrador puppy and named him "Lakota." Raising Lakota in her debilitated state pushed her to her limits, but she loved him so much that she accepted the accompanying pain and exhaustion, and eventually her condition started to improve more. She began walking with her dog a little farther each day and began to feel better. Being out in the woods was energizing and had a healing effect. Having a close bond with a dog again, and working with him, gave her a renewed since of purpose. Lakota was helping her to heal.

After seeing the healing effects he had on her, Margo thought Lakota could help others. After working with him, training and testing, Lakota became a certified therapy dog for a major organization, and Margo and Lakota visited hospitals and seniors, bringing joy into their day. After two years with Lakota, someone else's puppy came into their lives in an extraordinary way. That puppy was to change the course of Margo's life. The puppy, who came to her already named Zeak, also became a therapy dog. When the puppy developed a deadly cancer at only four years of age, an all-out battle with the disease ensued, and led to a profound spiritual experience as the dog was dying. Never having thought of being a writer, Margo plunged into telling the remarkable story of what had happened, and wrote, illustrated, and photographed—along with some photos from others—*Walking with the Shadow of Love: The Remarkable Story of Lakota and The Zeakie Dog.*

Continuing experiences with her dogs' spirituality plunged her into a fascinating new world. She found out that she was an animal empath (more about that in the Introduction) and began to understand things about herself that had puzzled her for her entire life. Lakota had passed, and now she was having contacts from both dogs.

After telling herself she would never have another dog because she couldn't bear to lose them, one afternoon a dog in need sent out an inner call she could not ignore. She rescued a beautiful but troubled dog and named her Kaya. Kaya's heartwarming recovery, incredible progress, and the bond she and the author now share, is a story in itself.

Other people started coming into Margo's life, people who had also had experiences with animal spirituality. As they shared their stories with her and as her experiences accumulated, she realized she had another story to tell, and wrote, illustrated, and photographed—along with some other photographers—another book: *Walking with Two Shadows: Real-life Stories of Love, Loss, and Reunion from Beyond the Rainbow Bridge.* Having personally experienced the profound pain that people feel when they lose an animal they have a deep bond with, Margo wants them to know that—even if they don't detect them—their beloved animals do go on in a different form. Those animals are around them and can hear them. They are with us to help and guide us, and they want us to live our lives fully.

Margo lives in New Jersey with her beautiful rescue dog, Kaya, and her two shadows: Lakota and The Zeakie Dog. She is now able to hike up and down a nearby mountain with them daily!

CREDITS:

The poem "Beyond the Rainbow Bridge" is an adaptation of the original "Rainbow Bridge" legend and was written by the author.

All photos and drawings by the author with the following notable exceptions, in alphabetical order:

Staci Ajello: photograph of Lakota in Chapter Twenty-Four.

Margo & William Bowblis: photographs in opening and closing composite pages.

William Bowblis: video capture photographs of Lakota (top left) and Cooper and Lakota (bottom right) in Chapter Ten, video capture photograph of Lakota in Chapter Eleven, photograph of Lakota in Chapter Twenty-One, photograph of Kaya in Chapter Thirty-Six, photograph of Margo and Kaya (bottom of author page).

Valerie Kerwin: photograph of Ainsley in Chapter Forty-Four.

Laurie E. Krauss: photograph of Kaya on opening and closing composite pages, photograph of Lakota (left) and Cooper (right) in Chapter Five, first and third photographs of Cooper and Zeak in Chapter Six, photograph of Cooper (left) and Lakota(right)—the second photograph in Chapter Sixteen, photograph of

Kaya in Chapter Twenty-Seven, photograph of Kaya in Chapter Twenty-eight, photograph of Kaya in Chapter Thirty, photograph of Cooper in Chapter Forty, photographic reference for author's drawing of Cooper in Chapter Forty-two, and photograph of Kaya on back flap of dust jacket (for hard cover only).

Cathy Lapenter: photograph of Carney and Van Gogh (top left) in Chapter Twenty-Nine (the light colored cat's name is first).

Kimiyasoo Mizoo: photograph for Chapter Twenty-Three, and photographic reference for author's drawing of Kaya in Chapter Twenty-Six.

Matt's Mother & Father...photograph of Matt in Chapter Forty-Five, and photographic reference for author's drawing of Matt and Daisy in Chapter Forty-Five.

Donna Riley: photographs of Flash in Chapter Four, and photograph of Willow in Chapter Twenty-Five.

Sheryl Spreen: photograph of Finnegan and Artemios (bottom right) in Chapter Twenty-Nine. (The light colored cat's name is first).

Samantha O'Neil: photographic reference for author's drawing of Izzy in Chapter Thirteen.

Sandra Struble: photographs of Lizzie (top left) and Bowie (bottom right) and photographic reference for author's drawing of Bowie in the epilogue.

Together. Together. Together.
We are everything.
We are everyone.
We are every thought.
We are every prayer.
We. Are. Love.

www.ingramcontent.com/pod-product-compliance
Ingram Content Group UK Ltd.
Pitfield, Milton Keynes, MK11 3LW, UK
UKHW062303290726
14090UKWH00017B/855

9 798218 088989